SUSAN JULIUS, Ph.D.

D0031471

SUSAN JULIUS, Ph.D.

Conversations
with
Preschool Children

A NORTON PROFESSIONAL BOOK

Conversations *with* Preschool Children

UNCOVERING
DEVELOPMENTAL PATTERNS

PAUL V. TRAD, M.D.

Director
Child and Adolescent Outpatient Department,
Cornell University Medical Center,
Westchester Division,
White Plains, New York

W·W· NORTON & COMPANY · NEW YORK · LONDON

Printed in the United States of America.

Library of Congress Cataloging-in-Publication Data

Trad, Paul V.
    Conversations with preschool children : uncovering developmental
patterns / Paul V. Trad.
        p.   cm.
    "A Norton professional book" – P. facing t.p.
    Includes bibliographical references.
    1. Interviewing in child psychiatry – Case studies.   2. Mental
illness – Diagnosis.   3. Life change events – Psychological aspects.
4. Preschool children – Interviews.   5. Child psychopathology – Case
studies.   I. Title.
    [DNLM: 1. Child Behavior.   2. Child Development.   3. Child,
Preschool.   4. Life Change Events – in infancy & childhood.   WS 105
T763c]
RJ503.6.T7 1990   155.4 – dc20   89-25531

ISBN 0-393-70085-2

W. W. Norton & Company, Inc., 500 Fifth Avenue, New York, NY 10110
W. W. Norton & Company Ltd., 37 Great Russell Street, London WC1B 3NU

1   2   3   4   5   6   7   8   9   0

CONTENTS

PREFACE

This book is designed to acquaint health-care professionals who work with preschool children with the astonishing
intricacy of the developmental process. Indeed, the underlying premise of *Conversations With Preschool Children: Un-
covering Developmental Patterns* is that "normal" developmental patterns can often be deceptive and misleading.
Behaviors that are suggestive of psychopathology may actually be entirely adaptive responses of a young child confronting such traumatic events as divorce, the birth of a new
sibling, caregiver separation, and the move to a new neighborhood. As these case histories reveal, only when the clinician possesses a rich and comprehensive understanding of
developmental events and the myriad of subtle effects they
exert on the child can an accurate diagnosis be made.

In order to assist the clinician in appreciating the complexities posed by development, several case histories are
presented in the following pages. Each case raises an important issue confronting the child during a vulnerable period in
his or her life. By exploring how the child confronts such
diverse challenges, I provide the reader with an intimate
view of development *in vivo.*

Each case depicts an episode in the life of a normal, adaptive child who is responding to the pressures and vagaries of
everyday existence. Nevertheless, in each instance the
child's symptomatology bears some resemblance to psychopathologic signs. It is my hope that by demonstrating the
often close resemblance of normality and psychopathology, I
will encourage health-care professionals to become more sensitive to the complexities of development and the need to
thoroughly examine the diverse factors affecting children.

ACKNOWLEDGMENTS

Several individuals were especially supportive during the germination of this manuscript. Among them were Stan Shaffer, Wendy Luftig, Stephanie Hill, James Wtorkowski, and Vernon Bruette, all of whom provided thoughtful critical commentary. My deepest gratitude is extended to Richard White for his unflagging support of my research efforts. I am also thankful to Craig C. Berggren, whose keen intelligence and insight have provided me with a new optimism for my future endeavors. Valerie Nea Shell was gracious enough to review portions of the manuscript and offer cogent observations. As always, my parents, Blanche and Jorge Trad, served as beacons of encouragement during the arduous process of preparing this manuscript.

Paul V. Trad
Cornell University Medical Center,
Westchester Division

Conversations
with
Preschool Children

1

DEVELOPMENTAL PSYCHIATRY

THE DEVELOPMENTAL PERSPECTIVE

Infancy and childhood are periods of rapid change, perhaps more rapid than at any other time in life. Within the rich and perpetually evolving self-system of a young child, emotions merge and behaviors overlap. Charting this volatile domain is the appointed task of developmental psychology. Specifically, the primary objective of those who approach psychopathology from the developmental viewpoint is to establish lines of predictive validity spanning from childhood to adult mental disorders and to demonstrate the nature of these disorders by describing the complementary interaction between internal states and external factors.

The purpose of this book is to provide the clinician with knowledge about the nature of development during the preschool era that will enable him or her to identify normal developmental phenomena that might otherwise be mistaken as psychopathology. The ability to discriminate between genuine psychopathology and age-normal developmental events will not only yield valuable information for devising an immediate course of treatment, but also prove indispensable for predicting the nature and likelihood of future difficulties. On a more ambitious scale, an understanding of the interrelationships between cognitive and emotional factors may facilitate prediction of future normalcy or psychopathology, even in the absence of overt manifestations of disorder. For these reasons, any clinician undertaking the psychiatric analysis of a young child's behavior is obligated to perform a parallel analysis of both the developmental factors and the psychopathologic manifestations affecting that behavior.

In attempting to achieve a model of intervention comprehensive enough to allow not only recognition but also prediction of maladaptation, developmental psychopathologists probe beyond specific behaviors to broader challenges facing individuals at different developmental periods. In addition to focusing on *disordered* behavior that actually manifests itself in childhood, the developmental psychopathologist also pays attention to *nondisordered* childhood behavior. By adopting this approach, he or she paints a more accurate portrait of the child's current level of adaptation, along with the prediction of which behaviors may produce later pathology.

Moreover, developmental psychopathologists are interested not only in the sequelae of a disorder, but in its precursors as well. Such a full range of interest requires an ambitiously eclectic approach, one that integrates knowledge from a variety of disciplines, including general developmental psychology, genetics, clinical psychiatry, embryology, developmental neurobiology, and physiology (Cicchetti, 1984). This eclecticism provides an inherent *flexibility*, a necessary ingredient when attempting to construct a discipline that has as its domain the full range and scope of human behavior. This domain carries with it the fundamental proposition that both normal and disordered individuals undergo a common course of development, with functioning at one level having predictable implications for later performance.

Let me emphasize that this developmental viewpoint is not the equivalent of a belief in behavioral stability. As Sroufe and Rutter (1984) have observed, coherence should not be confused with stability. Developmental psychopathologists expect that growth will result in behavioral *changes* as well as behavioral *continuities*. A belief in linear development has been abandoned in favor of a model that allows for the coexistence of behavioral transformations and regressions. While there is concern about the relationship between childhood and adult disorders, the developmental model specifically avoids "adultomorphism," the proclivity to focus on the similarities and overlook the differences between the child and adult forms of a disorder.

Just as adultomorphism is avoided, overemphasis on the nature versus nurture controversy is also guarded against. This dialectic has tended to oversimplify what is a very complex interaction between the constitutional dimensions of the individual and the external world. Developmental psychopathologists take into account the fact that individuals meet environmental challenges with diverse temperamental, as well as other biological, endowments. Neither "nature" nor "nurture" is favored in their analysis of development.

The multidimensional array of variables employed in the service of developmental psychopathology contributes to broadening the traditional medical model. Until recently, this limited model required that psychopathology be traced to an isolated, unresolved conflict from early life. By applying knowledge from all appropriate scientific disciplines to the many facets of development, the field of developmental psychopathology is in the process of providing the most all-encompassing picture to date of the nature and evolution of human behavior.

PRIMARY INVESTIGATIONAL CONSTRUCTS

Attachment Theory

That human beings are social animals is one of the oldest and most universal axioms of psychological theory. However, it was not until Bowlby applied the ethological viewpoint to this axiom that it began to yield useful revelations. It is now clear that from the very first day of life the infant's need to establish bonds with others is as compelling as the need for food (Bowlby, 1969). According to Bowlby, the main function of the attachment system is to maintain proximity to the mother. In ethological terms, this is analogous to protection from predators. Any disturbance in the environment alarms either the infant or the mother and brings them into physical proximity.

Running parallel to the attachment system is an exploratory system motivating the infant to move away from the mother and facilitating an adaptive exposure to environmental stimuli outside the immediate mother-infant framework. The infant's desire to explore and the mother's desire to maintain certain knowledge of her infant's whereabouts exist in constant dynamic equilibrium. When the infant strays too far, the mother becomes alarmed and makes efforts to retrieve the infant. Analogously, if the infant feels the mother is not within easy reach, it engages in behaviors that will reestablish contact.

Attachment behaviors that mediate the neonate's or young infant's relationship with the caregiver include smiling, looking, sucking, and reaching. These behaviors are designed to create and maintain contact. Bowlby (1969), Brazelton, Koslowski, and Main (1974), and others have described the familiar dialogue of back-and-forth coos, smiles, and babblings between infant and mother. These reciprocal interactions form the basis for the infant's first experiences of contingency relationships — and, therefore, of control (Trad, 1987). If the mother fails to respond in a consistent way to the infant's signals, the infant will experience a traumatizing sense of lack of control. If this pattern continues, the infant may develop a serious psychological disability, manifested by approaching all challenges with negative self-expectations — a situation that can quickly lead to depression and a variety of other behavioral difficulties.

These difficulties are clarified somewhat when Bowlby's attachment construct is applied to human infants in the "strange situation" developed by Ainsworth and Wittig (1969). In this experimental paradigm, infants are exposed to eight episodes that progressively tax an infant's ability to cope with the stress of separation from the caregiver. These episodes involve separation and reunion with the mother, as well as exposure to a new environment and to an unknown adult (i.e., a stranger). The infant is assessed in terms of reactions to the separation and the reunion, with the reunion behavior considered more important in categorizing the quality of attachment between infant and caregiver.

On the basis of observed behavior during the strange situation episodes, three basic groups emerge in relation to quality of attachment to the mother: A, avoidant; B, securely attached; and C, resistant. Avoidant infants display minimal desire for contact with the mother after separation. They show little distress when separated from the mother and treat a stranger in much the same way as the mother. Secure infants, on the other hand, actively contact with their mothers on reunion and exhibit marked distress during separation. Resistantly attached infants are a heterogeneous group, sharing a general quality of maladaptiveness. They are unable to use the mother as a secure base for exploration and revealed either distress or general passivity throughout the separation period. While further refinements of attachment categories have been established since the early trials of Ainsworth and Wittig, these basic categories serve to illustrate the usefulness of Bowlby's attachment theory when viewed through the strange situation. Infants who fail to receive sensitive, contingent mothering are at risk for developing negative and/or faulty assumptions about their own efficacy and roles in later life, since the dynamics and emotions generated during their first relationship with the outside world – their attachment to their mothers – will inevitably be applied to future relationships.

Since attachment theory allows observation of how adaptive and maladaptive behaviors are transferred from the relationship between mother and infant to other relationships in adulthood, it is one of the most valuable and fundamental tools of developmental psychology. As Bowlby (1988) has recently stated, " . . . variations in the way these bonds develop and become organized during the infancy and childhood of different individuals are major determinants of whether a person grows up to be mentally healthy" (p. 2).

Temperament and Self-regulation

The characteristic interaction between an infant and its mother provides a vital framework for understanding current and later adaptability. However, it would be a mistake to assume that this interaction is influenced solely by the actions and responses of the mother. The innate temperamental characteristics of the infant also make a significant contribution to the quality of attachment and to the individual's overall ability to cope. The infant becomes aware of its reliance on internal control when it begins to comprehend its separateness from the mother and from other elements in the environment as well. This threatening discovery initiates the lifelong drive for self-preservation through the mastery of challenges posed by the environment. If there is little or no ability to control internal impulses and drives, there will be no chance of achieving the moment-to-moment modulation of behavior necessary for survival in an ever-changing environment. Therefore, a major ingredient of temperament is the degree to which an individual is able to self-regulate moods and behaviors.

Another component of temperament involves the individual's level of reactivity to new stimuli from the environment. Rothbart and Derryberry (1981) define reactivity as: "... the characteristics of the individual's reaction to changes in the environment, as reflected by somatic, endocrine, and autonomic nervous systems" (p. 834).

A complementary definition of temperament, posited by Thomas, Chess, and Birch (1968) states that:

> Temperament is the behavioral style of the individual child – the how rather than the what (abilities and content) or why (motivations) of behavior. Temperament is a phenomenologic term used to describe the characteristic tempo, rhythmicity, adaptability, energy expenditure, mood, and focus of attention of a child . . . (p. 4)

Thomas and Chess argue that traits of temperament must be viewed along a continuum of "goodness" or "poorness of fit" with the environment. When there is goodness of fit, the likelihood of optimal development is enhanced because the individual is basically in step with the surrounding environment. Poorness of fit, on the other hand, produces dissonance between an individual's expectations and abilities and the expectations and demands of the environment. Poorness of fit can easily degenerate into distorted development and maladaptive functioning.

As examples, temperament (reactive style and self-regulatory ability) will influence the infant's ability to resolve discrepancies perceived in the environment and will also play a role in the infant's ability to perceive environmental contingencies and simultaneously to experience positive affect. Along these lines, Thomas, Chess, and Birch (1968) have identified three common types of temperament: "easy," "slow to warm up," and "difficult." The easy child is characterized by positive mood, regularity of body functions, adaptability, and positive approach. In contrast, difficult children exhibit negative mood, irregularity in bodily functions, and withdrawal from new stimuli. Slow-to-warm-up children are low in activity level, slow in adapting, mild in their reactivity, and have a tendency to withdraw from new stimuli.

SECONDARY INVESTIGATIONAL TOOLS

The reactive style and self-regulatory abilities of the child interact with the mother's behavior within the attachment relationship to form a system of development which can be analyzed using a number of subsidiary constructs. Among these are the development of cognition, play and prosocial behaviors, assumptions about locus of control, and the evolution of aggressive behavior.

The work of Einstein and Heisenberg in the realm of modern physics has emphasized the fact that reality is unavoidably observer-dependent. No universal standard exists against which one's reality can be nullified or verified. This fact makes the development of cognition a highly variable and volatile process, one that can provide a great deal of insight into a given child's degree of adaptability.

Cognitive development goes beyond the crucial tasks of mastering language and numerical reasoning. The ability to accurately perceive the internal processes of others, and thus their intentions, is also crucial to insure against the psychiatric difficulty labeled intersubjectivity (Trevarthen & Hubley, 1978). Inaccurate perceptions about the motives of others may lead to incorrect assumptions about the reasons for their behavior and about the causes underlying any number of other phenomena, not the least of which is loss or death. The developmental psychologist must take into account, for example, that the self-destructive behavior of a child may stem from depression, but it may just as easily be the result of faulty assumptions about the intentions of a relative who has died in combination with an incomplete understanding of what it means to be dead.

One useful way of making differential discriminations in such situations is to observe the child at *play*. Play is virtually the only means through which a child is first able to make and coordinate the all-important distinctions between appearance and reality. Play is also diagnostically useful in that it provides a reliable means of detecting pathology during childhood. Pathologic conflict or developmental deviation is suggested when the same play activity is repeated over a long period of time due to the inability to find a solution to the "play" problem posed.

Factors of temperament and attachment combine with cognitive development to form the child's most fundamental assumptions about himself. Does the child feel in control of surrounding events or has he or she adopted a passive posture, believing that whatever happens is basically beyond his/her control? Close examination of these *locus of control* beliefs yields valuable information about the general psychiatric health of the child. A child who believes that he or she is merely the passive recipient of environmental events is in danger of becoming depressed and of experiencing a reduced ability to cope.

Another dimension which may be used to assess a young child's behavior as normative or pathologic is that of *aggres-*

sive behavior. The developmental psychologist is aware of
the direct correlation between testosterone and aggressive
behavior, knowledge deriving from neuroendocrine research
and allowing assessment on a sex-specific axis from the outset. A developmental viewpoint also provides the realization
that where there is depression there is frequently aggression
born of the frustration of not being able to cope adequately
within the given environmental surroundings. This type of
eruptive aggression is considered hostile/destructive and is
extremely maladaptive in most situations. However, it is
adaptive in that it is directed at bringing down a system in
which the child is continually thwarted. Aggression of the
more normative variety, nonhostile/nondestructive, is simply engaged in for the purposes of testing the environment
and the reactions of others. The former type of aggression is
indicative of pathology, while the latter is not. Such distinctions are of obvious value when assessing developmentally a
child's troublesome behavior within the contexts of play and
prosocial behaviors.

DIAGNOSTIC VALUE OF
DEVELOPMENTAL PSYCHOLOGY

The developmental perspective can assist clinicians in for-
mulating accurate diagnoses, since an acquaintance with
normative trends of development will make them more sensitive to behaviors that are aberrant and thus indicative of
psychopathology. Understanding the progressive stages of
development provides a sense of what events occur during
which time periods in the course of normal development.

An example is the Piagetian system of cognitive development, in which a child progresses in gradual increments from
egocentric thinking to contextual and abstract thinking.
One manifestation of this process may be the finding reported in a study of preschool children by Kashani and Carlson
(1987) that the number of somatic complaints in association
with depression decreased with increasing age. Thus, a child
of nine or ten who is depressed and who also expresses so-

matic complaints may be experiencing a lag or deficit in cognition. Some investigators have hypothesized that such a delay in cognitive development may contribute to the etiology of depression in children (Trad, 1986, 1987).

Since a child's behavior is embedded in the overall context of maturation and development, affective problems should be viewed as either exaggerations or deficiencies of behavior patterns seen in children who are proceeding along the normal pathway of development (Plenk & Hinchey, 1985). Therefore, symptoms in children cannot be perceived as a set of adjectives that may combine to describe a discrete psychological state. Instead, such symptoms are more accurately interpreted as existing, to one degree or another, along the entire behavioral continuum that is available to every child. As a consequence, assessing psychopathology in the infant or young child is primarily, although not entirely, a matter of assessing the behavior in question in terms of intensity, frequency, and duration. To make these evaluations as precisely as possible, interviewing both the child and the parents and, if necessary, concerned individuals outside the family is essential. If an infant is involved, the clinician is encouraged to engage in interaction with the infant alone and to observe episodes of interaction between the infant and caregiver.

Above all, a comprehensive understanding of the patterns of both normative and abnormal behavior patterns is required. Armed with this knowledge of developmental trends, the clinician can use observational skills to formulate a differential diagnosis, ruling out certain conditions that may produce identical or related symptoms. Indeed, the developmental approach orients the clinician to consider virtually all the possible sources of psychopathology — from physiologic to purely environmental — prior to deriving a diagnosis. Because of this all-encompassing approach, following the guidelines of developmental psychology heightens the likelihood that a clinician will arrive at an accurate diagnostic profile of the infant or child.

CONCLUSION

The examination of the child's development using parameters of attachment and temperament and relating them to the development of cognition, play, locus of control, and aggressive behavior provides the most comprehensive approach for reaching meaningful diagnostic and prognostic conclusions. Of course, much work remains to be done, but, as Bowlby (1988) notes, the field of developmental psychiatry has in fact come of age. It may even be time to build a multi-axial, age-dependent system of developmental diagnosis starting with the early months of life and moving through childhood into the mature years.

2

DEVELOPMENTAL PERSPECTIVES FOR ANALYZING BEHAVIOR

The major facets of development during the preschool years are highlighted and interrelated here as we discuss the case of Steve, a five-year-old boy who aroused the concern of his teachers and parents by his overly rambunctious, sometimes apparently hostile behavior. Steve's actions and ever-shifting motivations will be viewed through a kaleidoscope made up of four observational lenses, each of which will transmit its own light of understanding about one or more aspects of his current and probable future behavior.

All four of the behavioral "lenses" described here—locus of control, aggression theory, cognitive theory, and play theory—will be discussed chapter by chapter in the upcoming pages. This introductory chapter is intended to provide a broad overview of the way developmental factors affect growth and the ways in which they can be used to discriminate between what is "normal" and adaptive and what is not at the preschool level.

STEVE

Five-year-old Steve comes from a large family in the lower-middle-income bracket. He has been referred for evaluation because his nursery school teachers have been unable to bring his behavior into the normative range for his age. Steve, whose father abandoned the family three years ago, is tall and above average in muscular build, and he exhibits a higher energy level than usual for this already energetic growth period.

Steve was interviewed first alone at the clinic and then with his mother. At the individual interview with the therapist Steve seemed very restless and eager to play. During the initial stage of the interview, it was difficult to engage him in conversation for any significant amount of time before he began protesting that he wanted to play with the toys in the interviewing room. Steve was expert at playing different characters as he ran about the room exploring. He soon began playing with a toy hunting knife he had hastily grabbed from the toy cabinet. This large rubber replica had a blade and a handle which he manipulated constantly, shoving it into his socks and shoes and waving it in the air as he spoke.

Steve was understandably reticent, and more than a little bored, talking to a stranger, but as time went on he began to drop his guard and speak more freely about his daily activities. Outside the nursery school setting, Steve often goes to the Boys Club in the afternoons and on weekends. When asked if he enjoyed the club, Steve's answer was, on the surface, somewhat unrelated to the content of the question. He related that there were four girls from his neighborhood who often played outside the Boys Club. Once, when they had persuaded him to let them borrow his bicycle, they had run away with it, leaving him to find it, somewhat damaged, two days later.

When asked how he felt about this incident, he said he was mad and would never trust those girls again, even though they sometimes spoke to him "inside his head" when they weren't physically present, trying to get him to do other things like give them money or bring them soft drinks. When asked how he felt when he heard these voices, Steve became visibly upset and angry, flourishing the knife and engaging in an energetic and surprisingly creative monologue about his wish to avenge himself. As part of his monologue, Steve mentioned how much he enjoyed watching television. The child informed me that he watched a great deal of TV, but that he liked the movies even better. The last movie he had seen had been particularly vivid and pleasurable to him. This turned out to be a very violent film with a strong "parental guidance" rating.

At this point, Steve's mother was called in. But before relating the events that followed, it will be helpful to describe the interrelationship of the four "lenses" that will be used to examine Steve's behavior and possible psychopathology. For reasons which will be explained, two of these theoretical constructs, locus of control and aggression theory, will be used to analyze the solitary portion of Steve's interview and the other two, cognitive developmental theory and play theory, will be employed to assess the interview that included Steve's mother.

OBSERVATIONAL LENSES

From the behaviors demonstrated by Steve during the initial observation session and from the comments of his caregiver, the clinician might be tempted to surmise some degree of psychopathologic response in the child. In particular, some of the behaviors manifested by the child are reminiscent of the symptom clusters listed in *DSM-III-R* under Oppositional Defiant Disorder, while other behaviors exhibited by this child appear to fall into the category of Adjustment Disorder with Work (or Academic) Inhibition.

In order for a child to be characterized as having Oppositional Defiant Disorder, a pattern of negativistic, hostile, and defiant behavior must be evident. In addition, such qualities as frequent loss of temper, arguments with adults, active defiance of adults in the form of refusing to do chores, deliberately annoying other children, angry or resentful behavior, and spiteful or vindictive actions must be present for a minimum of six months. Children classified with an Adjustment Disorder have been subjected to a psychosocial stressor that has occurred within three months of the onset of symptomatology. The most prominent symptom of this disorder is an impairment in functioning in the academic setting.

While the clinician may be tempted to assign one of the above labels after a brief review of Steve's history, a more considered determination is warranted here. While the child's play behavior during the initial observation was disordered and somewhat defiant, he was able to coherently communicate the incident involving the girls who had taken his bicycle. Moreover, while on first blush the comment about hearing voices in his head might be considered a sign of hallucinations, Steve's explanation of wanting to avenge himself made perfect sense.

The abundance of energy displayed by this child, when all the facts of his case history are considered, appears to be within the normal range. Steve's energy and aggression are understandable if we consider a couple factors: first, his father's abandonment of the family, an event the child may be having difficulty coping with regardless of the fact that he doesn't talk about it, and second, his recent experience of betrayal when peers took away a prized possession. The child's anger and frustrations are, therefore, entirely understandable and even expectable. Moreover, Steve's aggressive behavior here may actually be a sign of adaptation and healthy development, in the sense that he is striving to exert some control and mastery over events that appear to be uncontrollable, such as the departure of his father and the behavior of the girls in taking the bicycle. Acting-out through aggressive behavior may be this child's way of demonstrating his internal locus of control. Such activities may help make Steve feel he is a competent participant in a sometimes inexplicable and uncontrollable world and may actually function to stave off feelings of depression.

The interconnectedness of the four constructs can be demonstrated by looking at internal versus external locus of control. Locus of control provides a means of assessing whether or not current behavior is truly problematic in the sense that it may predict psychopathology in later child- and

adulthood. This construct examines the issue most fundamental to survival: Does Steve believe in himself to the degree that he feels in control of the majority of events that
occur in his life, or are his self-concept and feelings of power
so precarious that he assumes the opposite, that he is not in
control of the environment to a satisfying degree? The latter
assumption about the locus of control in one's life has been
associated with psychopathology, especially in the form of
depression (Dweck & Elliot, 1983; Peterson & Seligman,
1984; Tesiny, Lefkowitz, & Gordon, 1980).

Sackheim and Wegner (1986) have stated that perhaps the
most adaptive assumptions to make regarding the occurrence of life events (i.e., the individual's attributional style)
are: "If the outcome is positive, I controlled it, I should be
praised, and the outcome was very good. If an outcome is
negative, I did not control it (as much), I should not be
blamed, and it was not so bad anyway" (p. 558). One's assumptions about locus of control are intimately related to
the next construct to be used in assessing Steve, cognitive
development. Cognition is observer-dependent and the particular observer bias (internal or external locus of control)
derives from the ability to form mental representations of
self and others—an ability which depends upon the quality
of the relationship with the caregiver, the original "object"
from whom the child differentiated himself.

The context in which the child develops his cognitive and
emotional abilities is the arena of play. It is through play
that the child exercises maturational skills, moving from life
according to the pleasure principle to life based on the reality principle. And of course, very little will happen in the way
of personality development unless the child has access to his
own internal drives and is able to assert himself in the pursuit of satisfying these drives. Parens (1979) has pointed out
that assertiveness or aggression is a healthy component of
personality as long as it is nondestructive or nonhostile,
meaning that it is not directed at destruction of the self, the
object, or the environment. Nondestructive aggression is directed at mastering the many challenges that arise through-

out development. Hostile destructive aggression, on the other hand, is directed at eliminating structure and is driven by excessively felt displeasure such as occurs with strong feelings of insecurity.

STEVE'S LOCUS OF CONTROL

Q: Who stole your bicycle?

A: (frowning and shifting restlessly in his seat) The girls.

Q: Did they take it when you weren't looking?

A: No. Sheila asked if she could ride it.

Q: And you said OK?

A: Yeah.

Q: Then what happened?

A: (indignantly) Then Sheila got on and rode around the building but didn't come back and then the other girls pushed me down and ran away.

Q: Why did Sheila steal your bike? Doesn't she like you?

A: I don't like her!

Q: Do you think Sheila would have stolen your bike if you had said no when she asked to ride it?

A: No! She could never get it if I didn't let her!

Q: Would you let me borrow your bike now, if I promised not to hurt it?

A: No!

This exchange reveals something of Steve's inner assumptions about the degree to which control emanates from himself vs. external sources. Discovering whether or not Steve has an internal, positive belief about his ability to control some events in his life will provide a good fundamental index of his risk of psychopathology. If he believes he is mostly in control of what happens to him, he will be likely to feel the world is a good enough place. If, on the other hand, he feels put upon by events beyond his control, he will be poorly equipped to cope with life's events.

Perhaps the most fundamental aspect of locus of control is the fact that the development of the self is a function of the infant's expanding regulatory system. Since self-regulation and self-control are closely related, the characteristic way in which the child attempts to control himself and his environment *becomes* the child. These adaptational modes reflect the origins of a recognizable personality.

Rothbaum, Weisz, and Snyder (1982) point out that control involves bringing the environment into line with the individual, as well as bringing the individual into line with the environment. Therefore, adaptation can be defined as understanding how and when to apply each form of control. Children who fail in the attempt to gain control over their emotions and impulses are at as much risk for psychopathology as those who fail to achieve a feeling of control over their environment.

Since Steve was referred for overly impulsive, at times aggressive, behavior, we can speculate that he is experiencing problems in controlling his inner urges. Furthermore, his inward fantasies—or hallucinations—of being told to do things by the girls in his neighborhood suggest an invasion of the self from outside. The invasive feature of the voices may in fact be more important in terms of risk for psychopathology than the fact that he is having hallucinations per se, since evidence is mounting that hallucinations in childhood are not that uncommon (Rothstein, 1981; Schreier & Libow, 1986).

Steve's sense of control has been shaken by the traumatic experience of losing his bicycle to the girls. We might ask whether his external locus of control is more global and attributed to events in the world at large. One way to examine this issue is by assessing the level of Steve's motivation, his desire to keep striving to control environmental factors and events. If Steve has reached a point where he feels events are largely out of his control, his motivational level is likely to be low. This occurs for much the same reason as animals eventually fail to attempt escape after repeated shock in a learned-helplessness situation (Seligman & Maier, 1967): Being repeatedly subjected to episodes of helplessness when confronted with environmental challenges causes the animal/individual eventually to become habituated to the experience of helplessness and undermines the motivation to strive for mastery.

While it certainly appears that Steve has work to do in terms of regulating both internal urges and external responses, his motivation to conquer the environment remains high. This is an encouraging sign. Not only does he recognize the fact that he had some initial control over the bicycle incident ("She could never get it if I didn't let her"), but he also shows determination not to relinquish control a second time by refusing to loan his bike to me. With proper guidance, Steve has a good chance of learning the necessary lessons about control – for the simple reason that control brings mastery and Steve is highly motivated to attain mastery.

ANALYSIS OF STEVE'S AGGRESSIVE BEHAVIOR

Q: What do you do when one of your friends is crying?
A: I try to make him feel better.

As already mentioned, there are two fundamental types of aggression: destructive/hostile and nondestructive/nonhostile. The former, being directed at the annihilation of structure, is indicative of psychopathology, since it suggests a desperate, last-ditch effort to escape a wholly untenable life situation. The difference between the "good" and "bad" types of aggression is really only a matter of degree, since aggression in general is always spurred by frustration (McDevitt, 1985). The greater the degree of frustration in such ego pursuits as exploration, mastery, and coping, the more likely the development of destructive aggressive activities.

Aggressive impulses begin to emerge early in development, achieving their most urgent levels during Mahler's rapprochement subphase of development beginning around 18 months. During this developmental phase, the infant struggles to establish a consistent identity in the face of the encroaching awareness of being separate and individuated from others. Contributing to the awareness of one's separateness is the fact that at this time the child must also function and develop in the face of fears of object (mother) loss and of losing the object's love (Mahler, Pine, & Bergman, 1975).

Because this period is so charged with anxiety and frustration, there is a high risk for the development of destructive aggression. In the absence of a strongly developed self that can confidently perform actions on the environment, much of this aggression may be shunted inward into the unconscious, where it is manifested in fantasies, or directed physically against the self in the form of "accidents" that may not actually be so accidental (McDevitt, 1985).

In later sessions it was established that Steve had no history of accident-prone behavior, a positive sign in terms of his ability to handle the many difficulties surrounding the separation-individuation or rapprochement phase of development. Nevertheless, the potential for frustration (and consequent aggression) remained great for Steve even after the completion of this difficult developmental phase.

Steve's marginally impoverished environment in and of itself may be associated with increased levels of frustration-driven aggression (Dodge, Pettit, McClaskey, & Brown, 1986). In addition, as a male Steve is inherently more prone to aggressive behavior than a female child (Maccoby & Jacklin, 1980). Then, of course, there is the abandonment of Steve and his family by his father—a traumatic separation experience over which Steve had no control at all and around which he undoubtedly experienced much frustration and pain.

Another factor contributing to a potentially exacerbated level of aggressive acts is the fact that Steve has three siblings, all boys, the oldest of whom continually teases him, calling him names and surprising him with not-so-gentle "mock" physical attacks. While it is true that aggressive behavior is most common in the family setting, and especially so among siblings, it is also true that the presence of sisters in the family (or females in the peer setting) serves as an inhibitor of aggression. With no sisters and Steve's busy mother, often at work, there is very little in the home environment to oppose the occurrence of aggression.

Steve's aggressive tendencies are also fueled by his protracted television watching and by his exposure to violent movies. In the absence of an adult mediator to explain the intentions and severity of the actions seen on the screen, children are very likely to internalize some of the behaviors (including aggression) they see performed by adults (Ellis & Sekyra, 1972).

The finding that television can give rise to increased levels of aggression in children – and that this process can be interrupted by the intelligent, caring intervention of an adult mediator – illustrates the fact that empathy, the accurate perception of the intent of others, is perhaps the single greatest inhibitor of aggressive behavior. The capacity for empathy, or affective perspective-taking, has been observed in children as young as 18 months (Zahn-Waxler & Radke-Yarrow, 1982). Some of these very young children even changed strategies if their initial attempts at offering comfort to a distressed peer failed.

If he lacked the capacity to differentiate his own intentions from those of others, Steve would be able to interpret the behavior of others only in terms of external physical events. If this were the primary source of his aggressive behavior toward peers, Steve would be at grave risk not only for increased volatility as time goes on, but also for increased social isolation and reduced mastery. However, it is doubtful that this is the case. Steve was easily able to identify the intentions of his capricious girl peers and to invent pretend characters during play sessions, revealing good ability for affective perspective-taking combined with the ability to express a wide range of emotions and affective responses, all of which have been observed to be strong contributors to the development of prosocial behaviors (Feshbach, 1979).

Since the general ratio of prosocial versus antisocial aggressive behavior has been observed to carry over from the family to the school setting, it seems likely that Steve is simply following the norm for behavior which has developed in his home. As discussed, the norm for aggressive behavior in Steve's home is far in excess of the overall norm for society. While this is unfortunate in the sense that Steve will have some difficulty bringing his behavior in conformity to the age norm and achieving peer acceptance, it is not as difficult a problem as it might be if there were more deep-seated reasons for his aggression.

STEVE'S COGNITIVE DEVELOPMENT

Q: Did the alien get him? (pointing to an action figure that had been "shot" by the aliens in one of Steve's game scenarios)

A: Yeah.

Q: So he can't play anymore?

A: (matter-of-fact) No. He's dead.

Q: But would it be OK if he just had something to eat but didn't play anymore?

A: Well, OK.

Before discussing the broad contributions to disordered behavior of incompletely developed cognitive ability at the five-year-old level, let us return to the interview room to meet Steve's mother. The conversation with Steve and his mother was followed by a period of play.

Steve seemed happy to see his mother when she entered the room and sat in a chair beside him. However, discussion between the two quickly centered on a recent episode between Steve and his older brother, who often teased him. This particular occurrence involved an accidental closing of the bathroom door on Steve's hand as he tried to sneak up on his brother. The discussion centered around whether or not it was really an accident and upon the fact that Steve's mother had laughed at the incident. Steve appeared to be upset that his mother would laugh at something that hurt him and was worried that perhaps his mother joined with his older brother in conspiring against him from time to time. Steve's mother assured him that she did not approve of the way his older brother treated him but added that she had to laugh because it looked so funny when the door hit his hand. Although Steve did not seem entirely satisfied, he accepted this answer. Throughout the rest of the conversation, Steve and his mother were alternately playful and serious. While they appeared to get along well enough, their mutual affection did not extend to the point of touching each other at any time – a fact that might be explained by mutual inhibition in a strange place with a strange person.

When one of his many requests to play was finally granted, Steve ran to the toys and began almost immediately to play imaginatively. He took a toy car off the shelf and ran it through a gaggle of female dolls, swerving at the last second to avoid hitting them. He denied one of them permission to go for a ride and then picked up a toy gun and started playing a different game called "get the alien," dodging around the backs of chairs and firing from between the legs. Steve showed no interest in the more passive, structured games that were available (e.g., Lego).

To fully comprehend the nature and level of Steve's cognitive development, it was essential to have some idea of the nature of Steve's relationship with his mother. Understanding the character of the early attachment relationship between the two, as reflected in current interaction patterns, is valuable in assessing Steve's personality development. A very young child must use the mother as a base from which to explore. Optimally, the mother represents a "secure" base, which promotes growth and exploration (Bowlby, 1969).

Stress of any kind activates this mother-infant action system, causing the child to seek proximity to the mother. If the relationship with the mother is not secure, but instead is infused with anxiety (e.g., the mother gives the infant ambivalent signals when it explores by providing encouraging vocalizations when it leaves and showing disapproval upon its return), this will act as a source of stress and cause the infant to reduce efforts at exploration. Consequently, children who are anxiety-prone and in anxious relationships with their mothers will explore relatively little and will be handicapped in their mastery of the environment (Trad, 1986, 1987).

As the child continues to develop, he or she explores through play activities, eventually developing cognitive sophistication. Thus, we see that the quality of the early attachment bond affects the enthusiasm underlying exploratory/play behavior, which in turn directly affects the quality of cognitive development.

Fundamentally, cognitive development entails the progressive ability to make distinctions between appearance and reality—not only in terms of physical appearances but also in terms of the outcome of others' actions and the intent behind those actions (i.e., was the outcome intentional or accidental?). Inaccurate perceptions of the motives of others may lead to fallacious assumptions about the reasons for their behavior and about the causes underlying any number of other phenomena (e.g., accidental versus intentional injury). Here, too, the quality of the attachment bond plays a pivotal role. If the mother and infant have a secure relationship, the baby will experience minimal stress in breaking away from its identification with this first "object" and establishing its own being in the world. If, on the other hand, the relationship is insecure, the infant will feel threatened each time it attempts to break away, and this will delay and/or cripple subsequent attempts to discriminate between self and another.

Along these lines it appears that Steve is fairly age-normal in terms of comprehending the intentions and reactions of others. He accurately interpreted the actions of the girls as being intentional when they took his bicycle, even though he trusted them in the beginning, and he was justifiably upset when his mother laughed at him after he was hit on the hand with the bathroom door. These disclosures indicate that Steve's cognitive processes are rational and that he is capable of understanding cause-effect or contingency relationships in an objective fashion. He does not make distorted attributions that would indicate a disturbance of locus of control perceptions.

However, it would be unwise to assume too great a sophistication in terms of comprehending intentionality in Steve's case, as revealed by the fact that he thought maybe a dead person could still come to dinner. Among other things, children under six years of age are generally unable to differentiate between luck and skill (Nicholls & Miller, 1985). Nevertheless, Steve seems well on the way to developing a sound sense of intentionality – a functional ability that will guard him from erroneous assumptions about the actions of himself and others and hence inhibit inappropriate aggressive responses.

This assessment suggests that the original attachment bond between Steve and his mother was sufficiently secure to allow him to form accurate and appropriate mental representations and affects based on separation from her, the first appearance-reality distinction of his life. Further elements of Steve's cognitive capacity will emerge with an examination of his play situations.

STEVE AT PLAY

Q: You really like to play, don't you?
A: (enthusiastically) Yeah!
Q: What kind of playing do you like best?
A: Soldiers and nurses!
Q: Do the nurses ever argue with the soldiers?
A: Sometimes.
Q: So sometimes the nurses don't help the soldiers when they're hurt?
A: Once she didn't, but he got OK anyway.

Various types of pretend/play activities, ranging from simple fantasy to role-playing, provide the developing child with an arena in which to practice appearance-reality distinctions through assimilation and accommodation, the two major processes involved in cognitive development (Piaget, 1962). There are three basic components to play as children practice it: (1) expression of wishes and fantasies; (2) enactment of those wishes in an attempt at fulfillment; and (3) awareness of the nonreality of the play situation (Neubauer, 1987).

The fact that play demands enactment of situations and events is what provides the clinician with a communicative and therapeutic link with the child. This is a very valuable characteristic of play activity, since children lack the verbal skills to completely convey their internal state. It is also through play that a child can act against what has been passively accepted in real life, providing an opportunity for distancing and an immediate mechanism for coping with as yet unmastered situations (Fein, 1981; Fink, 1976; Freud, 1932). In short, scaling down thoughts to the level of symbolic play enactments or pretend episodes, such as refusing to take the girl doll for a ride, allows Steve to begin to master feelings associated with a traumatic situation.

The more immature the child's symbolic abilities, the more real-life situations promote play in an attempt to gain perspective and mastery. Conversely, real-life situations inhibit play in the presence of more mature representational abilities (Hulme & Lunzer, 1966; Piaget, 1962; Watson & Fischer, 1977). The fact that Steve was so anxious to begin playing suggests a strong need to master his feelings about the way the girls mistreated him and to prove to himself that he will not soon find himself in a similar situation.

Play provides a means of coping with traumatic occurrences as well as a means of organization, allowing the child to connect language with imagery storing processes. In fact, play may be the single most important means of allowing the systems of language and images to interact on the way to forming accurate reality constructs that combine with flexible internal emotional states (Rohwer, 1967; Singer, 1973).

Thus, it would seem that Steve's eagerness to play from the outset of the interview represents an adaptive tendency to master his strong feelings of violation of trust, particularly with regard to the incident with the girls and his bicycle, which is very much on his mind. While Steve does have numerous risk factors for expressing violence (aggression), the underlying indicators for subsequent psychopathology (e.g., insecure attachment bond, poor motivation, external locus of control) do not appear to be present.

If Steve's aggressive milieu (unsupervised television and

movie watching, aggression by his brothers, aggression among peers in his lower-middle income neighborhood) can be improved, Steve's behavior will likely reach the point where his prosocial behaviors outweigh his antisocial activities. This is particularly likely if Steve is able to come to terms within himself about various traumatic incidents, an eventuality that will be facilitated by psychotherapy.

CONCLUSION

Although the behavior of this child during the intake interview, coupled with his case history, suggested that incipient psychopathology might be present, thorough investigation of the child's perceptions through observations of play behavior indicated that Steve was behaving adaptively for his developmental level.

This case history demonstrates that aggressive tendencies that emerge during play episodes need to be carefully examined by the clinician. The clinician should first strive to obtain an explanation for the aggression from the child himself or from the case history. In this instance, one event in the case history provided an explanation for some of the child's aggressive tendencies. Abrupt departures of one parent from the home can understandably unleash anger and frustration that is manifested in the form of aggressive behavior. In addition, however, this child was able to provide another inherent explanation for his aggression. The story about the girls who took his bicycle seemed to dominate his thoughts as he enacted aggressive gestures in front of the clinician.

Although, as indicated, the behavior of this child mandates that he be followed, a developmental assessment reveals that Steve's aggression may in fact represent an adaptive means of coping with and exerting control over unpleasant experiences in his short life. The child's cognitive capacities should be monitored to ascertain whether future development will allow him to resolve his anger and frustration in even more adaptive ways.

3

COGNITION

Evidence that a preschooler has a tendency to engage in accident-prone behavior is always cause for concern by the clinician. It is vital that the differential diagnosis of such children include the possibility that such "accidents" are *not* accidents at all, but are instead intentional acts on the part of the child that are designed to cause injury to himself and others. As will be discussed in this chapter, the cognitive status of the preschooler can sometimes operate in an insidious fashion to cause the child to ignore the full ramifications of his actions.

ROB

Rob is a mature-looking three-and-one-half-year-old who, on first appearance, seems quiet and introspective. However, after he becomes acclimated to a new situation or environment, his activity level increases markedly — virtually to the point of impulsivity. His IQ tests reveal a score in the high-normal range.

Rob's parents brought him in for evaluation on the recommendation of his pre-kindergarten teacher. They, too, have been concerned about their son for some time because of his tendency to have accidents. His father, a well-paid tool and die maker, and his mother, who stays at home, have recently moved with Rob from a rural area on the outskirts of Kansas City to the highly urban setting of New York City. Since the move four months ago the frequency of Rob's accidental events has increased noticeably, according to his parents. In spite of the fact that he is under almost continual surveillance by an adult, Rob has had a number of close calls since moving. His mother once found him standing outside on the window ledge of their 14th-floor apartment, and his preschool teacher became alarmed when she encountered him wrapping tape around the face of a playmate. In another incident, the teacher turned around to see that Rob had erected and climbed a six-foot tower of play blocks placed on a desk and was about to jump, holding a toy cloth parachute over his head.

Rob's parents appear to get along well, and both are concerned about their only child's behavior. Rob's mother states that her son has always been "active" and that in his case the "terrible twos" were truly terrible.

When questioned about these incidents, Rob typically shrugs and turns away, seemingly puzzled by all the fuss. His feelings about death are understandably vague, given his age and cognitive abilities. Questioned about what he thought would happen if he jumped from the apartment's window ledge, Rob smiled and simply said, "Fly!" When pressed and told that he wouldn't fly but instead might fall and hurt himself, or even die, he responded that he just wanted to play, and besides, everybody got hurt sometimes and died. But, it was explained, sometimes when you get hurt it can't be fixed and you can't play anymore; you can't do anything anymore because you are dead — that's what being dead means. In response to this, Rob smugly contradicted himself and replied, "Not everybody gets hurt. I could still play!" In light of his potentially self-damaging behavior, Rob's parents were persuaded to bring him in the following week for a more extensive evaluation.

The child in this case, Rob, appears to be oblivious to the meaning and consequences of self-destructive acts. This is illustrated most vividly in his inability to comprehend that death is an irrevocable process, applicable to all, that completely ends life. Because of Rob's high activity level during the evaluation, parental reports of accident-prone behavior and his apparent cognitive confusion over the meaning of death, the clinician may initially posit the presence of psychopathology. Two likely diagnoses from *DSM-III-R* that might encompass some of the child's symptomatology include: Attention-deficit Hyperactivity Disorder and Parent-Child Problem. With respect to the Attention-deficit Hyperactivity Disorder, Rob has a tendency to fidget, his high activity level makes it difficult for him to remain seated, and he is easily distracted by extraneous stimuli. Most notably, he often engages in physically dangerous activities without considering the possible consequences. All of these behaviors fit criteria for Attention-deficit Hyperactivity Disorder.

However, in Rob's case, other factors need to be carefully evaluated before such a diagnosis is made. For example, the clinician must consider that the family's recent move to an urban environment from a rural area may have upset and confused the child. A change of this type may be especially unsettling to a preschooler who is just beginning to grasp the cognitive concepts of permanence and immutability. Moreover, as will be seen, Rob's immature notions of death are age-appropriate; preschoolers generally fail to understand the finality and irreversibility of death.

Nevertheless, while Rob's cognitive level of development may help explain why he fails to understand the ramifications of his actions, this cognitive immaturity does not negate the fact that the child could inadvertently hurt himself. As a consequence, this is a classic example of a case in which normal adaptive behavior should be monitored. The child's apparently innate level of hyperactivity, coupled with what may be unexpressed feelings about the family's move, could create a dangerous situation.

COGNITION AND SEPARATION

"There is only one real person in the world, and that person is me." This aphorism aptly portrays Rob's egocentric viewpoint and that of every very young child. He feels himself to be an undifferentiated part of the environment, omnipotent and carefree, and governed by rules that can change from moment to moment according to his whim and perhaps even his control. The statement also gives warning of the difficult task ahead: the building of internal systems of logic and emotion that will protect the integrity of the individual who must coexist with others, each of whom is living in accordance with his or her own, different definitions of reality. As Rob and his parents are discovering, the task of learning to live and work together is perhaps the most difficult of all tasks because, while no two persons' perceptions of reality are exactly the same, it is ultimately impossible for any of us to prove or disprove our sense of things.

Despite the impossibility of building a completely accurate internal representation of reality, the human organism is compelled to make the attempt. Around the age of two there is a sudden and stark realization that what has been conceived as being "reality" is in fact a sham. The onset of consciousness (the perception of a self separate from all else) forces the young child to realize that, instead of being inextricably connected to a whole and complete world, he or she is in fact *not* at the center of all things. The ensuing sense of being powerless and set apart from the environment at large gives rise to anxiety about survival in much the same way as anxious feelings arise upon separation from the caregiver.

The entire course of life from birth to death can be charted as a series of separations. First the infant moves from the meta-attachment to the environment at large, which is intrinsic to the feeling that he or she is indissoluble from the surrounding world, to the separation from that world that occurs with the first stirrings of consciousness (the perception of a "self" separate from other things). Concomitantly, with the increasing drive for autonomy, the child must withstand another frightening separation—this time from his or her mother or caregiver. Finally, as a child and adult the individual encounters numerous separations—leaving home, death of loved ones, or divorce, to name but a few. Eventual-

ly we all confront one final, ultimate travail: death, the separation from life itself.

How one copes with these and other life traumas is dependent upon the sophistication of the individual's cognitive
and emotional faculties. While mastery of language – which
Rob is well on the way to achieving – and numerical reasoning are cognitive tasks important for survival, the ability to
accurately perceive the internal processes of others, and
thus their intentions, is perhaps even more important for
insuring against psychiatric difficulty. Inaccurate perceptions of the motives of others may lead to fallacious assumptions about the reasons for their behavior and about the
causes underlying any number of other phenomena (e.g., accidental death vs. suicide).

The picture worsens when an inadequate empathic ability
to attribute intent is combined with an incomplete cognitive
understanding of the nature of death – a combination that
exists during childhood, especially the early years. These
bimodal deficits in emotional and cognitive comprehension
contribute to the fact that accidents are the major cause of
death in children (McIntire, Carol, & Strumpler, 1972). Children like Rob, with immature empathic and cognitive abilities, fail to fully appreciate the three properties associated
with being dead: universality, dysfunctionality, and irreversibility. Furthermore, young children also fail to realize that
death can have natural, accidental, and intentional (suicide
or murder) causes.

With regard to Rob, what must be determined is whether
his accidents are merely the result of immature cognitive
and empathic abilities combined with an impulsive nature,
or whether these "accidents" are intentional manifestations
of a wish to hurt himself or to "die" – a desire to avoid conflict
and enhance coping by achieving a different state of being
whose characteristics he does not fully understand. The latter possibility raises the question of whether or not Rob
suffers from a disorder such as depression that has weak-
ened his representational abilities and thus his sense of self
and the implications of his behavior. Therefore, assessment

will focus on both the cognitive and the emotional/empathic (ability to comprehend intentions of self and others) dimensions of his current state of development.

COMPREHENSION OF INTENTIONALITY

Q: Do you know how your mom feels about you?
A: She loves me.
Q: Yes, she does. Do you know what that means?
A: (with great conviction) It means she loves me.
Q: And does that mean your mom would never hurt you, even by accident?
A: Yeah.

As the child comes to realize that others do not think exactly as he does, he makes attempts to adapt himself to this fact, acquiescing to the realities of control and verification (Piaget, 1927). Along the way, however, the child is likely to encounter several pitfalls which may or may not permanently disorganize his cognitive development. It is likely that Rob has stumbled into one of these.

First, however, we need to determine whether or not Rob is seriously depressed and at immediate risk of taking his life through self-destructive behavior. As mentioned in Chapter 2, children with an internal locus of control are likely to believe they can act to overcome adversity, while those with a predominantly external locus of control feel they are at the mercy of outside events. Children in the latter group are at greater risk of developing depression because they believe they are at the mercy of powerful forces outside of themselves (Abramson, Seligman, & Teasdale, 1978; Seligman & Peterson, 1986; Zautra, Guenther, & Chartier, 1985).

It quickly became apparent in subsequent sessions that Rob had a very strong sense of self and equally strong feelings about being able to control his environment. This quality correlated well with an optimistic anticipation for positive outcomes, flexible internal attributions for positive life events, and adaptive patterns of social interaction which he

approached with persistence. Therefore, on the broad indicator of locus of control, and judging from his demeanor in
general, Rob did not appear to be depressed or in any immediate danger from himself – at least *intentionally*.

However, he may still be at risk for eventually developing
depression since, as Seligman and Peterson (1986) have
found, a mixture of internal locus of control and a preponderance of negative outcomes (e.g., accidents) is a fairly strong
predictive combination for depressive affect. The negative
impact of this combination is exacerbated by Rob's imperfect understanding of intentionality, evidenced by his belief
that his mother would never hurt him, even accidentally. Not
only might negative outcomes be self-attributed, but he may
also make the mistake of assuming that accidental slights
from his parents are in fact intentional.

Intentionality Defined

As defined by Shultz (1980), intention refers to "a mental
state that guides and organizes behavior. It is essentially a
determination to act in a certain way or to bring about a
certain state of affairs" (p. 131). The studies of Piaget (1952)
strongly suggest the presence of intentionality in human
infants, but the degree to which infants are actually aware of
an intentional state is still unknown.

The ability to understand and attribute intentionality is
strongly related to the child's nascent capacity to form mental representations of himself and others in his world. These
cognitive abilities regulate the interpretation of the child's
own behaviors and of the primary people in his/her life – in
addition to determining whether or not self-destructive behavior will result from stressors such as parental psychopathology, abuse, or parental death. For instance, abused
children might feel responsible for and/or match violence
inflicted upon them if they confuse their own intentions with
those of their abusers. Furthermore, the child of a parent
who committed suicide might act out his own self-destructive urges when confronted with a confusion about inten-

tionality. Fortunately, Rob is not an abused child, nor is there a history of suicide in his family.

Another problem that may develop as a result of a poorly developed sense of intentionality is what Weisz (1981) describes as "illusory contingency." This involves a mistaken perception about the nature of causality in relation to an event or a class of events. For example, an externally caused event is mistaken for one that is within the purview of personal control or under the control of another person. Also, the level of control that is actually available is generally misperceived. Since Rob's accidents have been contextually unrelated, it seems doubtful that he has developed a dangerously erroneous assumption about the outcome of a certain action. Of course, his assumptions are erroneous about his vulnerability to dangerous situations in general.

In children five to six years old, Kuhn (1977) identified a "magnification co-variation" schema. This was characterized by the belief that the degree of success at a given task was attributable to a change in the degree of ability or effort and was *not* related to any external factor such as task difficulty. This schema is similar to an "attributional schema" developed by Nicholls (1978), the "halo" schema. Nicholls observed that children five to six believe that a positive outcome is directly attributable not just to effort or ability but to both. Thus, under this system – which Rob is unlikely to have developed as yet because of his age – greater effort is associated with greater ability.

More pertinent to Rob's case are the findings of Nicholls and Miller (1985). Studying causal schema, they found that children under six years of age do not differentiate between luck and skill. Only with age do these factors diverge and obtain separate attributions. This finding perhaps relates to that of Seligman and Peterson (1986), who found that nondepressed children tend to attribute positive outcomes to internal causes and negative outcomes to external causes. Depressed children, in contrast, do not make this distinction and therefore are at risk for developing deficits in self-esteem, which in turn exacerbate their negative affect. Paradoxically, Rob's especially powerful sense of internal locus of control (which may prove resistant to later modification), in combination with the high incidence of accidents, may combine to increase his chances of later developing depression. How is he to reconcile his sense of control with the bumps and bruises that follow his daredevil actions?

Timing of the Acquisition of
Intentionality

The sooner a concrete sense of intentionality develops, the sooner the child is protected from erroneous assumptions about his own actions and those of others. In his review of the field, Shultz (1980) found that by age three children *can* distinguish intended actions from unintentional behaviors such as mistakes, reflexes, and passive movements. About the same time, the ability to recognize sequential relationships develops. Although some researchers believe children aged three to four cannot comprehend causal orders (Kuhn & Phelps, 1976; Piaget, 1929; Shultz & Mendelson, 1975), other researchers argue the opposite (Bullock & Gelman, 1979; Kun, 1978).

Piaget (1929) reports that young children tend to juxtapose events based upon their spatial and time proximities; children may believe that effects precede causes, for example. Shultz and Mendelson (1975) argue that children perform co-variations (Kelley, 1973) when making cause-and-effect distinctions; that is, children may attribute effects to any one of a possible number of co-variates. For example, the young child may believe that wood burns because it is in the fireplace; if the wood were not in the fireplace, it could not burn. The researchers found that three-year-old children used co-variation information in order to create causal schemas; in addition, they often attributed effects to co-variations that followed the effects themselves. The investigators posit that three-year-olds are incapable of temporal ordering and may structure causality based upon recency effect, attributing the effect to the most recently occurring co-variate.

These findings might be cause for concern in Rob's case; after all, if this three-year-old cannot understand causality, he will not appreciate the possible consequences of his risk-taking behaviors. However, studies by Bullock and Gelman (1979) and Kuhn, Nash, and Brucken (1978) suggest another perspective. They discussed investigations in which children were called upon to communicate concepts that they may have understood but lacked the communicative expertise to verbalize. Often, it seemed to the researchers, the children in these studies were not provided with sufficient information to allow them to verbalize their comprehension. When these investigators designed studies carefully controlling for these factors, it was found that the causal assumptions of three-year-olds are indeed based upon temporal ordering cues. Thus, while children may be unable verbally to communicate their cause-and-effect assumptions, that does not mean that they lack an understanding of the sequential nature of events. In light of his high IQ, it seems unlikely that Rob is having difficulties in making these distinctions; rather, his undeveloped language skills may hinder his ability to express and convey his perceptions to others.

It is not until age five, however, that the child is able to see the difference between intending an act and intending a consequence (Shultz, 1980). By this age children are also able to realize that others are aware of intentions, as revealed in efforts to disguise their own intentions from others.

Learned Helplessness

It is within the arenas of intentionality and locus of control that the child is at potential risk for learned helplessness. In this model, the individual perceives himself as being unable to control or master events (Abramson et al., 1978). These feelings of uncontrollability rapidly produce anxiety and depression—so quickly that they may well develop during the first months of life if the caregiver fails to create a sufficiently harmonious relationship for the infant. The child who has experienced a high degree of negative affect from birth may be extraordinarily vulnerable to depression by the age of two when the sense of self begins to consolidate.

Even if, as in Rob's case, the child experiences a relatively normal environment, he/she may view foreseeable outcomes as being more intentional than those that are unforeseeable. Thus, concepts such as death may seem remote to a child and may not be incorporated to any great extent into the developing child's representation of the world. This condition, when combined with the self-oriented thinking of children, clearly places the child at emotional and physical risk due to poorly evolved notions of intent and outcome.

It appears that Rob's level of development in terms of intentionality, while understandably immature, is at least comparable to that of other children in his age group. He demonstrates normal assumptions about the good intentions of his mother and appears to be functioning well with his peers, despite his sometimes overzealous play. Furthermore, his strong internal locus of control is actually somewhat advanced for his age. While it is true that he may be at risk for developing depression in the future if his accidents continue, he does not appear depressed currently. Therefore, it seems unlikely that his accident-prone behavior is attributable to a significant impairment in the comprehension of intent.

COGNITIVE DEVELOPMENT AND COMPREHENSION OF THE DEATH CONCEPT

Q: Does everyone die?
A: Yes.
Q: So, you'll die someday, too?
A: No!

Rob's comprehension of the nature of death (including its components of irreversibility, universality, and dysfunctionality) must be evaluated; first, however, let us compare his overall cognitive development to date with some established norms.

In his treatise on the child's conception of physical causality, Piaget (1927) argues that any causal explanation is dependent upon the degree of cognitive development involved as well as upon the extent of subjective awareness the child might have of certain specific causal relationships. When analyzing the way children describe the manner in which things happen around them, Piaget developed the descriptive construct of *indirect egocentrism*, that is, the world is assimilated to such an exaggerated extent that properties of the self are assumed to be properties of the environment as well. One example of this is *animism*, in which children assume that, for example, because clouds move they are alive, just as the child is alive. However, the child does not assume that all the properties of the self are incorporated in the environment. Experimentation and deduction exist very soon after decentering (i.e., after the onset of consciousness), and only certain properties of the self are attributed to the universe based upon these cognitive effects, rudimentary though they may be (Gruber & Voneche, 1977). In the attempt to define reality as children conceive it, over stages of development, Piaget describes it as "what the biologists call environment" (p. 129 of Gruber & Vaneche, 1977). In other words, the environment – its objects and the relationships between those objects – come to be related to each other in a system shaped by the innate biological qualities of the individual.

The child's understanding of the environment is accomplished by a simultaneous progression away from realism along three dimensions: *objectivity*, *reciprocity*, and *relativity*. By realism, Piaget (1927) meant the primal state of mind in which the child's consciousness exists undifferentiated from the external world; i.e., there is no distinction made between the "I" or self and the environment. When the child's cognitive capacities are at this developmental stage, psychic phenomena such as dreams are given physical properties and vice versa.

The progression from this undifferentiated state of realism to objectivity is simply one in which the primal state of consciousness divides to form two cognitive sets, the subjective and objective universes. It is important in analyzing the development of the death concept, or any other aspect of cognition, to note that a state of complete objectivity is impossible to attain. Piaget describes five distinct classes of "adherences" (portions of internal logic and experience that never become completely dissociated from the external world, making full objectivity unobtainable): (1) *feelings of participation*, such as when clouds are believed to follow our movements; (2) *animism*, in which life-like qualities are attributed to inanimate objects; (3) *artificialism*, embodied in the belief that surrounding objects take notice of us as individuals as well as of fellow human beings, and that everything is organized for the good of man; (4) *finalism*, in which relationships are viewed from an anthropocentric viewpoint, as when a child believes bicycles move in order to let people ride them; and (5) *force*, the assumption that objects have wills of their own, with their efforts fueled by energy similar to that used by muscles.

In moving from realism (egocentrism) to reciprocity, the child gradually comes to realize that points of view other than his own do exist. Thus, instead of what is immediately obvious, reality is taken to be the common ground between the points of view perceived by various individuals. In other words, a child might realize that, while a motorcycle is heavy to him, it is less so to an adult.

The concurrent movement from realism to relativity is similar to the movement towards reciprocity. As the child progresses to relativity he or she sees objects as being more and more dependent upon other objects. In other words, he or she sees them as being relative to one another. As Piaget (1927) notes, all three progressions away from realism take place simultaneously, develop slowly, and are never totally completed. They appear to be interdependent and continue throughout the life of the adult. Therefore, concept formation is a labile process; definitions are subject to change at almost any point in time, depending on experience, temperament, and psychosocial stressors. The lability of concept formation is evident in Rob's contradictory statements about death. Initially, he stated that everyone died (the universality component), but then he said that he would be able to play even if he were dead (failure to comprehend the dysfunctionality aspect of death.)

The effect of temperament on cognitive development is far from trivial. In Rob's case, with his impulsivity and noticeably high activity level, temperament may in fact be playing a major causative role in his accidents. Klein and Tzuriel (1986) assessed 72 kindergarten children on the basis of several different measures of vocabulary, memory, and reasoning and classed them as belonging to one of the three types of temperament categories developed by Chess and Thomas (1984). These categories are (1) the easy child, characterized by high exploration and adaptability, regularity of body functions, mildness of response, and positive mood; (2) the difficult child, displaying negative mood, arrhythmicity, intensity of response, and low adaptability to new people and new situations; and (3) the slow-to-warm-up child, who displays low activity level, variable rhythmicity, mild intensity of response, and negative mood. In Chess and Thomas' studies, the difficult and slow-to-warm-up children were at risk for developing psychiatric disorders.

Klein and Tzuriel found no differences between the three temperament groups on vocabulary measures or reasoning tests. However, the difficult children scored significantly lower than the other groups on measures of immediate sequential memory. This impairment of memory was found to be most strongly related to distractibility and intensity of response in the difficult group. Thus, children with difficult temperaments may be susceptible to cognitive deficits.

While Rob does not appear to fall completely within the definition of the difficult child, he does possess attributes of both the difficult child (intensity of response) and the easy child (high exploration). Furthermore, he is highly impulsive and experiences arrhythmic bursts of energy contingent upon these impulses. The properties of impulsivity and intense responsivity tend to disorganize (desynchronize) Rob's attempts to build a reality construct during his numerous exploratory episodes – a process which may be hampering his perception of the causal relationship between dangerous actions and death. Thus, his understanding of causality and the properties of death may lag behind that of, say, a child with an easy temperament. Here we have the first hint that Rob's accidental behaviors may be associated with cognitive deficits rather than with his comprehension of intentionality.

With some understanding of Piaget's general conceptions about the development of a reality schema, we can begin to examine the stages of cognitive development and relate them to Rob's developmental level and perceptions about the three facets of the death concept. While Piaget stressed the simultaneity and interdependence of the fundamental processes marking the path away from egocentrism/realism, he formalized his findings by describing a gestalt of cognitive development embodied in three sequential stages (Piaget, 1929, 1948).

Soon after the child is able to perceive objects as being apart from self, he or she enters the *preoperational* subperiod of thought, primarily by acquiring the semiotic function, that is, the ability to represent something outside of the self by means of a signifier, such as a gesture like pointing or a verbal sound. At this stage, the adherences of animism, finalism, and artificialism are most prevalent (Greenspan, 1979).

By definition, the preoperational subperiod is marked by an inability to perform operational thinking, that is, thinking that aligns reality according to internalized, consistent systems of action which are viewed as being reversible. Under such cognitive constraints, roughly between the ages of three and six, the child's ability to manufacture symbols and learn signs which represent his/her experience is far in advance of the capacity to understand them in a socially integrated way. This is clearly the case with Rob, whose actions show very little inhibition resulting from social interactions.

The gap between concept formation and social testing

generates the greatest degree of egocentric thinking. With little basis in reality, assumptive philosophies about the operation of people and the world are formed. During this stage, "magical" thinking is at its zenith (Elkind, 1976) and, as demonstrated by his case history, Rob was no exception to this trend. At the same time, the child believes there is only one reason, with no possibility of arbitrary events, leading him to assume that his highly imperfect perceptions of reality are hard facts. Furthermore, an assumptive philosophy, nominal realism, evolves, in which it is believed that the name of an object is an essential part of the object – objects can neither be changed nor separated from their names.

Along these lines, Rob is an inveterate pointer and object namer. According to his mother, he first engaged in this process at around 18 months of age. He clearly seems to be functioning at this preoperational level; consequently, he has probably established numerous "assumptive philosophies" that he is attempting to test – another factor predisposing him to accidents. Making matters worse and compounded by the limitations of this level of cognitive development is his recent relocation from a rural milieu, in which he had already developed ways of testing a familiar environment, to an urban setting, where many of his exploratory techniques and established assumptions about reality are no longer workable. The resulting frustration in testing new hypotheses may be adding fuel to his inherent tendency toward arousal and impulsiveness.

It is important to note that the development of assumptive philosophies occurs at approximately the same time as Mahler's rapprochement subphase of separation-individuation (Mahler et al., 1975). Thus, it appears that the development of the child's capacity for mental representation may trigger not only the realization of dependency and vulnerability in the surrounding world, but also the beginning realization of separation from the caregiver. Anxiety and/or depression from this double trauma very likely overshadows the development of the understanding of death. Since the response to the burden of figurative thinking is frequently a regression to egocentrism, the child may use the same defense when faced with the notion of death, a concept requiring that he or she face the prospect of separation—not just from the caregiver, which is traumatic enough—but from life itself. While I am speaking theoretically here, it may be that at least part of Rob's initially serious and introspective demeanor is reflecting his struggle with this issue.

With the advent of *concrete operational* thinking, the child is able to evaluate the relative permanencies of properties over the course of change, i.e., he or she is able to conserve. Whereas a child in the preoperational subperiod will believe a liquid changes in quantity if it is poured from a short, wide glass to a tall, narrow one, a child employing concrete operations will reason from the viewpoint of the configuration of the glass and perceive that there has been no change in the volume of the fluid.

In other words, operational thinking incorporates the ability to reason about transformations, a task Rob has yet to master. This emergent ability may provide the first path leading away from egocentrism precipitated by separation anxiety before and during the preoperational subperiod. If things can transform from one essence to another, the child (and even the adult) retains the hope that the same will be true for him—even in the case of death. Thus, even when Rob enters the concrete operational period, chances are that he will still fail to fully comprehend all aspects of death.

During concrete operational thinking, the child forms assumptive realities to replace the assumptive philosophies of the previous stage. If a preschooler (three to six years) is presented with a finger maze, he will immediately place his finger on the maze and work it through by trial and error. On the other hand, a child employing concrete operational thinking (roughly between ages seven and eleven) will attempt to solve the puzzle visually before placing his finger in the maze. During this period, the child develops an enhanced cognitive capacity to understand the ramifications of intentionality.

However, cognitive operations are still incomplete at the

concrete operational stage. As mentioned, an understanding of the death concept may remain incomplete within the context of concrete operational thinking, since there is still confusion about reality of mind versus matter. This is the result of the fact that, while the child may be able to conceive of a course of action, he or she is still largely unable to test it immediately.

Around the time of puberty, children begin to assess reality along the axis of the real versus the possible (Flavell, 1963). In this, the most mature stage of thought, experimentation and logic are applied to all the possible relations that might exist in order to discover what *does* exist. Whereas assumptive realities allowed the conception of possible courses of action, *formal operations*, or *assumptive psychologies*, enable the child to view his hypotheses as just that — hypotheses. In so doing, he can test and experiment with these hypotheses in the world.

This operation also allows the adolescent to form clearer representations of his own feelings and thoughts, as well as those of others. However, adolescents commonly make the mistake of assuming ideas are shared when in fact they are not. As an example of this confusion, many adolescents have difficulty conceptualizing their own death and feel that they will live on while everyone else in the world may die. Thus, failure to comprehend the universality component of death may persist into adolescence. Despite such limitations, there is a greater freedom from the immediate content of things within formal operations periods. This serves to generate an increased intellectual mobility. Abstractions not only can be formed, but can also be manipulated regardless of whether or not they are associated with a concrete event (Greenspan, 1979).

In terms of the evolution of the ability to make an accurate distinction between appearance and reality in any given situation, Flavell, Green, and Flavell (1986) sum it up in the following manner. Compiling the results of seven studies with children in different age groups, these investigators found that the majority of three-year-olds possess very little discriminative ability in terms of reality vs. appearance. Children six to seven years old are able to solve both appearance/reality tasks and perspective-taking tasks but have difficulty explaining how they do it. Secure ability does not appear until the age of eleven or twelve and does not fully develop until college age.

EVOLUTION OF THE DEATH CONCEPT

Q: When did you find out that everyone dies?
A: (shrugs) I don't know.
Q: If everyone dies, that means you could die too.
A: If I did I could still play.

The ways in which children approach the issue of "separation from life" (i.e., death) can have a profound impact on the risks inherent in their playful exploratory behaviors. In light of the fact that accidents are the foremost cause of death in children, it seems likely that an incomplete grasp of the nature of a "death outcome" plays a significant part in disinhibiting the actions of the very young child, an organism already imbued with rampant energy and curiosity. Thus, in assessing Rob's case it will be clinically valuable, as well as theoretically instructive, to apply the dynamics of cognitive development to the evolution of the comprehension of death.

In order to assess the development of children's comprehension in this regard, the various elements involved in the concept must first be defined. In an extensive evaluation of 122 white middle-class male children between three and twelve years of age, Kane (1979) tested comprehension of ten components inherent in the reality of death:

(1) *Realization* was defined as the awareness of death or of the state of being dead as happening to a specific person.

(2) *Separation* pertains to the location of the dead (e.g., underground).

(3) *Immobility* concerns the child's ideas about the movements of the dead (totally inactive or partially or completely mobile).

(4) *Irrevocability* pertains to the child's notion of death as either permanent and irreversible or only temporary and reversible.

(5) *Causality* is defined as a belief as to what brings about the state of death — either internal or external causes or a combination of the two.

(6) *Dysfunctionality* relates to conceptions about bodily functions other than the senses. From the child's perspective the dead may be either totally or only partially dysfunctional.

(7) *Universality* is a measure of ideas relating to mortality. Children may believe everyone dies, no one dies, or that there are exceptions.

(8) *Insensitivity* pertains to mental and sensory functions (dreaming, feeling, thinking, hearing, etc.). The child may view the dead as being totally without sensation or partially or completely sensate.

(9) *Appearance* deals with the conceptions of the way the dead look.

(10) *Personification* refers to whether or not death is regarded as a person or a thing.

In this study, children as young as three years of age were found consistently to understand at least some components of the death concept. By age four, all the components were detectable in varying degrees. By age seven, except for the dimension of appearance, most children were able to represent all components. By the age of eight, almost every subject was seen to understand every component but appearance, which became fully integrated by age twelve.

Kane's results are in general concurrence with Piaget's model of cognitive development. During the preoperational stage, death was conceptualized as obvious and in the present, containing three principal components: realization, separation, and immobility. These components clearly demonstrate the advent of decentered thought. While they were held concurrently, they were not seen as related to one another. During the second subperiod, death was seen as concrete and specific. It was an explanation (hypothesis) for dysfunction. In stage three, death was conceived in abstract terms, and the children speculated as to causes and consequences (formal operations).

Kane's results are a refinement of those of Nagy (1948), who was the original investigator in the area of the child's conception of death. In studying 378 children, Nagy found three stages of development in the meaning of death to a child. As we have seen, children like Rob in the three-to-five-year age group do not see death as final and believe in degrees of death. Between five and nine years of age, children personify death. According to Nagy, only children older than nine or ten have a mature outlook regarding death. Thus, as Nagy depicts the situation, Rob would be expected to be disinhibited in his actions by his failure to recognize death as a state of permanent dysfunctionality – a normal developmental proclivity for a child of his age.

In their review of the literature regarding normal children's comprehension of death, Speece and Brent (1984) found that the majority of healthy children in Western industrial societies obtain an understanding of death between the ages of five and seven. The discrepancy between their findings and Nagy's may result from experimental refinements or reflect a general trend toward earlier and earlier decentering in response to the surrounding world's ever increasing social and technological complexity.

In their analysis, Speece and Brent (1984) condensed the various components of death into three principal concepts: universality, irreversibility, and nonfunctionality. In the studies they reviewed, young children were often reported to understand death as temporary and reversible. Before completely grasping nonfunctionality, children view death as being different from life in such a way that dead things do not have all the functional possibilities of living matter; for example, a child may believe that dead people cannot hear as well as living ones. Regarding death's universality, children are first likely to believe that they can avoid death, as Rob demonstrated, or that some classes of people are immune from the effects of dying.

In an attempt to identify the sequence in which a mature understanding of death is achieved, Speece and Brent note that the possibilities encompass: (1) the concurrent acquisition of the three components deriving from a base of cognitive achievement or (2) independent acquisition in either (a) an invariant sequence or (b) a variant sequence. While there was a wide range of ages of acquisition in the studies reviewed by Speece and Brent, the finding that all three components appeared to be understood between the ages of five and seven led the two investigators to hypothesize that the components may all be acquired concurrently. This is especially compelling in light of the fact that, according to Piaget (1952), five-to-seven is the period during which children move from preoperational to concrete operational modes of thinking.

The confluence of conceptual understanding is also reflected in studies attempting to relate the acquisition of the different components of the death concept with the stages of cognitive development. For example, White, Elsom, and Prawat (1978) selected 170 children between the ages of three and ten from three public schools in upper-, middle-, and lower-class suburban neighborhoods. Individual interviews were conducted with each child. In the first part of the interview, the children were given three conservation tasks relating to conservation of substance, of continuous quantity, and of discontinuous quantity. These tasks were taken directly from the concept assessment kit of Goldschmidt and Bentler (1968).

After completing the conservation tasks, which tested the ability to comprehend transformations, the child was moved to another station in the testing room and was read a very short story by another investigator. There were two versions of the story. One version portrayed an elderly woman as being kindly to her pets and to little children. In the other version, the woman was portrayed as mean and unlikeable. Each version of the story was read to half the students of each age group. Following the reading, each child was asked general questions, including, "Do you think that everybody will die someday?" When a child responded affirmatively, a preplanned follow-up question requested an explanation. Conversely, if the child answered negatively, he or she was asked to name someone who would not die and someone who would. The concepts were judged to be correctly understood only if an affirmative response was followed by a logical justification. Twenty-two percent of the children who heard the unkind woman version of the story attributed her death to some "bad" action she had performed; of the children who heard the kind woman version, only one attributed her death to some action of hers.

Interestingly, while these investigators did find an increase in the child's comprehension of universality attributable to cognitive development, they found no relation between the other two components – irreversibility and nonfunctionality – and cognitive development. White et al. (1978) point out that this may be explained by a distinction made by Vygotsky (1962) between spontaneous and scientific concepts. According to Vygotsky, spontaneous concepts are gained through intuition. Thus, universality may be a spontaneous concept, while irreversibility and nonfunctionality are more scientific or intuitive in nature.

In this regard, White and coworkers note that this notion gains further credence from Piaget's (1948) work relating to moral judgment. Piaget found concrete operational thinking to be related to belief in the absoluteness and universality of rules. Thus, universality in general appears to be a spontaneous concept, generated from within the child's own urge for structure – as demonstrated by Rob's partial recognition of death's universality. It may be a keystone to further cognitive development, in relation not only to the comprehension of death but also to the comprehension of the environment at large.

CONCLUSION AND FINAL ASSESSMENT

The way in which we come to judge our circumstances in life, as well as the manner in which we respond to life experiences, depends greatly upon what we feel, what we think of ourselves, and the manner in which we conceptualize our environment. While this may seem to be stating the obvious, the task of understanding the developmental dynamics of cognition underlying these processes is extremely difficult. The fact that there seems to be no easily identifiable sequence to the acquisition of the various cognitive components of the death concept illustrates the diverse heterogeneity inherent in the development of cognitive processing. Nevertheless, comprehension of developmental hallmarks such as separation-individuation, along with awareness of the major cognitive risk factors for psychopathology in relation to self-esteem, locus of control, and attribution of intent, can greatly assist the practitioner in performing a clinical assessment.

In conversation and during play activities, Rob demonstrated a healthy quest for unifying principles, as evidenced by his partial comprehension of the universality of death. He understood that death exists and applies to everyone and also grasped other "universals," such as all carrots are orange and all mothers are girls. However, it was quite apparent that the property of death was a variable thing for this child, applying to some people some of the time and existing in varying degrees of severity.

As discussed, these misperceptions are common for a child of his age. Were it not for a recent separation trauma (moving from a rural to an urban area more than a thousand miles away) and his energetic, impulsive nature, they would not pose any grave danger. However, with Rob's temperamental characteristics and history of accidents, the age-normal failure to fully comprehend the implications of his acts when he engages in dangerous behavior only adds fuel to the problem.

Pertinent to Rob's case are Schneidman's (1966) three exploratory types in relation to accidents among children: the death darer, the death chancer, and the death denier. If these characterizations apply, Rob would appear to be a death chancer, eagerly and impulsively exploring his environment in an anxious attempt at mastery in the face of a "death" that, from his perspective, probably won't be permanent and may not even hurt much. His development is expected to proceed normally as long as he is watched closely. His parents must be encouraged to be patient and vigilant until their son learns more about his new urban environment, himself, and the nature of death.

What is notable about this case, then, is that a combination of factors that are due to the normal processes of cognitive maturation — the natural energetic tendencies of a three-and-a-half-year-old boy and immature notions about the implications of self-destructive acts — have combined with an external situation in the child's life — the move to a distinctly new environment — to create a case profile that suggests psychopathology. Rob's most alarming behavioral manifestation is his accident-proneness, and in other situations such accident-proneness should alert the clinician to possible abnormality. Here, however, this disturbing behavior seems to have emerged as a result of the normal processes of development.

Rob's behavioral profile necessitates that he be carefully monitored to insure that the processes of cognitive development continue. It will also be helpful to explore more fully, through play and other forms of enactment, how the child is experiencing the move. It should be emphasized that, while Rob's failure to understand the implications of self-destructive acts may be due to a naturally expected cognitive deficit that will vanish over time, his accident-proneness may be attributable to other factors that have aroused his anxiety, anger or fear. As a result of the stimulation of these emotions, Rob may be "acting out" in a fashion that will attract the attention of not only his parents but also the new peers he is encountering at school. It is recommended, therefore, that Rob's parents be coached in methods of reassuring their son that the move is now complete and does not pose a risk to the stability of family life. Most likely, only if such reassurance is given by the parents will the child be able to begin exerting control over behaviors resulting in repeated and unecessary accidents.

4

LOCUS OF CONTROL

This case highlights an issue – separation-individuation – which many believe to be instrumental in the development of a secure and stable sense of self. Although researchers have pinpointed two years of age as a key time in the development of a coherent sense of self, as the child accomplishes separation-individuation from the caregiver, in actuality the issues of separation and individuation dominate the course of childhood. It is incumbent upon the clinician, therefore, to examine the degree of stability the child exhibits with respect to sense of self and secure relationship with the caregiver.

LISA

Lisa, an exceptionally attractive and vivacious four-year-old, was brought to the clinic by her parents. From the beginning of the evaluation, Lisa's behavior was highly energetic and ingratiating, but somewhat disorganized. For example, when a stranger inadvertently entered the room, Lisa lost her train of thought and seemed to become confused and unhappy. However, for the most part, she skillfully managed to contain her energy, keeping her behavior just short of being unruly and disruptive. The majority of the time, she was extremely charming, taking an interest in the therapist's choice of tie and slacks and finding other effective ways to be flattering. However, her parents were noticeably excluded from many of her attempts at ingratiation.

Both mother and father expressed deep concern about their daughter, but their overall demeanor—not merely as it pertained to their daughter—was somewhat removed, as though a significant portion of their attention was focused elsewhere. Lisa's parents have been divorced for approximately one year, but both work for the same company, he as an electronics design engineer, she as a computer specialist. Both are enthusiastic musicians, practicing flute and cello as much as two hours a day. Lisa is their only child.

While her parents are no longer living together, they share equally in their concern for their daughter. Lisa lives with her mother in the house where she was born. Her father lives three miles away and takes her to school (first grade) each day. Both parents describe their divorce as being non-traumatic and equitable. As they put it, "We grew apart and thought it best to end the marriage, but Lisa belongs to both of us." The marriage terminated shortly after the couple arrived back in the United States from an extended trip abroad, during which time Lisa was left in the care of a nanny whom she hadn't met previously. This occurred when Lisa was two and a half and ended with her third birthday.

In the year since, Lisa has exhibited an increasing tendency to defy the orders of her teacher and parents and to show fairly rapid mood swings. The impetus for bringing Lisa in for evaluation came from her teacher, who notified her parents of an increase in problem behavior (e.g., refusing to share play items, striking her playmates, and throwing tantrums when frustrated). The concern of both parents seems to be centered primarily around their daughter's future academic performance; they fear that her schooling will suffer if her behavior does not change. Her mother is especially concerned that "the problem" be resolved soon, since her company is sending her overseas in six months to supervise installation of the computer system for a new manufacturing facility. While she is away, Lisa will live with her father in his nearby apartment.

When this plan was being discussed by her parents, Lisa became subdued and placed her head in her father's lap while her arms hung limply at her side. Then, abruptly, she straightened up and ran over to the doll shelf. She selected a stylishly dressed female doll and said, in a sing-song voice, as if imitating someone, "If you try really hard to be a good girl while I'm gone, maybe I'll come visit you when I come back!" Following this statement, she replaced the doll very gently and stroked its hair. At this point, Lisa's mother called her over. Lisa scowled, hesitated, and then complied, primly sitting in her mother's lap and eliciting a hug.

The remainder of this initial session was spent discussing Lisa's many achievements. She attended a preschool for advanced children, read at the second-grade level, and was showing great promise as a violinist.

Lisa's case is of great interest because it highlights an issue which many believe is instrumental in the development of a secure and stable sense of self. This is the issue of separation-individuation. Although researchers have pinpointed two years of age as a key time in the development of a coherent sense of self, as the child accomplishes separation-individuation from the caregiver, in actuality the issues of separation and individuation dominate the course of childhood. It is incumbent upon the clinician, therefore, to examine the degree of stability the child exhibits with respect to sense of self and secure relationship with the caregiver.

THE PAIN OF SEPARATION

From some of the information obtained during Lisa's initial interview, separation appears to pose a problem in this child's life. She has already been subjected to two separations with potentially traumatic consequences. The first involved her parents' departure to Europe on a trip. This separation may have had a debilitating effect on the child – first, because of her age at the time of the separation, and second, because both of her caregivers left her. The second separation, the parental divorce, may have been equally debilitating to Lisa. At the tender age of three years she was forced to confront the notion that her parents didn't get along with one another. Given Lisa's level of cognitive development, such a realization may have triggered a variety of responses. First, she may have self-attributed the breakup of her parents' marriage. In other words, given the status of her cognitive abilities, Lisa may have viewed the divorce as being her own fault. Or, Lisa may have been traumatized by the event in the sense that she came to believe that one or both parents might abandon her permanently.

Behaviors resembling genuine psychopathology included lack of playfulness and failure to respond to social interaction; these suggested Reactive Attachment Disorder and Phase of Life Problem. As will be seen from the ensuing discussion, Lisa's developmental status was, in fact, normative for her age level. The disturbing behaviors that had prompted an evaluation arose primarily as an adaptive response to another episode of separation from her caregiver.

Q: How do you feel when you think about your mother's leaving?

A: I wish she wouldn't go (Lisa lowers her head, continues softly). It makes me sad.

Lisa's unhappiness and anxiety, as well as her skillful prosocial attempts to compensate for or conceal these feelings, were evident at the time of initial assessment. Lisa is experiencing an understandably high level of anxiety over the impending separation from her mother – an anxiety which is probably compounded by the experience of two previous separations in her life. Lisa experienced separation from her parents when they went to Europe and partially when they divorced. What must be determined is whether Lisa carries with her a continuous sense of sadness and anxiety severe enough to impair her adaptive learning ability or whether her depressed affect is largely attributable to the prospect of being separated once again from a parent.

One productive way of approaching the assessment of a child like Lisa, whose emotional and behavioral problems may or may not foreshadow later psychopathology, is to ex-

amine what is perhaps the child's most fundamental assumption about herself: Does she feel in control of the events
around her or does she feel herself to be a passive recipient of
life's uncontrollable alterations? If the latter is the case, Lisa
will be at risk for developing a debilitating level of depression
(i.e., persistent feeling of powerlessness) (Johnson & Sarason,
1978; Peterson & Seligman, 1984; Trad, 1986, 1987).

The reason for the increased risk of depression in those
who lack a feeling of personal, or internal, control is straight-
forward: Attitudes influence feelings, which in turn shape
behavior. In a cyclical process, the results of behavioral efforts at control modify attitude and affects. If the attitude
toward one's own efficacy in the world is predominantly one
of powerlessness, actions taken by the individual will not be
performed with conviction. The lack of confidence dampens
the efficacy of the individual's coping responses, producing
less than successful results and further reinforcing the sense
that power comes not from within but from without.

Thus, the developing child's attitude about his or her locus of control (LOC) – that is, whether control of events originates internally or externally – is an important component
of the psychological profile. In Lisa's case, a close scrutiny of
her locus of control beliefs will provide a strong measure of
her difficulties and the degree to which they are likely to
confound future attempts at adaptation and coping. The history of her own negotiation of the separation-individuation
process – and her exposure to separation shortly afterwards
when her parents divorced – would seem to place Lisa at risk
for developing feelings of powerlessness. On the other hand,
her words to the doll suggested a strong desire to master the
situation – a positive sign in terms of adaptive ability.

The strategy of using Lisa's locus of control beliefs to
assess her psychological state derives substantial support
from the literature. A great many investigations into the role
of perceived control have demonstrated its usefulness in
evaluating patients at risk of developing psychopathology,
depression in particular (Abramson et al., 1978; Dweck &

Elliot, 1983; Johnson & Sarason, 1978; Peterson & Seligman, 1984; Rotter, 1966; Seligman & Maier, 1967; Tesiny, et al., 1980). The association between a weak sense of internal control and debilitated coping capacities has been further substantiated by studies that show these individuals to have a higher correlation between stressful life events and psychopathologic symptomatology (Denney & Frisch, 1981; Husaini & Neff, 1981; Lefcourt, Miller, Ware, & Sherk, 1981). Additionally, people who feel that they lack primary control over the environment have reported a variety of symptoms suggestive of depression, including passivity, sadness, anxiety, lowering of appetitive drives, neurochemical deficits, and susceptibility to disease (Peterson & Seligman, 1984).

Clinical concern about a person's perception of control is further justified by the fact that beliefs about the degree of control one exerts over events have been found to be a persistent facet of personality, resistant to change, and applicable to a wide range of phenomena (Hegland & Galejs, 1983; Galejs & Hegland, 1982). By preschool, children may have well developed beliefs about the degree of control they have, beliefs which shape many of their interactions with significant people in their environment (Galejs & Hegland, 1982). Since the competence with which children interact with others at a very early age has been demonstrated to predict many types of competence later in childhood, attitudes about controllability, which may influence the success of these early interactions, are likely to be important markers for future adaptive ability (Arend, Gove, & Sroufe, 1979).

Beck (1963) first observed in depressed patients a number of recurrent themes betraying a negative bias toward the patient's perception of the self. These included low self-regard, ideas of deprivation, self-criticism and blame, the sense of overwhelming problems and duties, helplessness and hopelessness, escape and suicidal wishes. Beck found that depressed patients frequently distorted reality by attaching negative connotations to any activity that could reflect on their abilities or personality. They interpreted events

with this negative self-bias even when the evidence contradicted their interpretations.

The automatic, involuntary, and persevering nature of
their distortions led Beck to conclude that cognitions play a
significant role, interacting with affects in the development
of depressive symptoms. Although he did not attempt to
determine whether depressive thoughts precede depressive
affects or the other way around, he did suggest that the
interaction of affects and cognitions could create a continuous cycle of distortion. Cognitive assessments of the self as
being alone, alienated, or unworthy could, for example, lead
to feelings of sadness, loneliness, or guilt. Conversely, loneliness might lead to lowered cognitive assessment of the self.

Since Beck made these observations, many researchers
have isolated specific areas of cognition associated with depression both in adults and in children (Abramson et al.,
1978; Beck, 1963). Although *DSM-III-R* categorizes all
forms of depression as "Affective Disorders" — reflecting the
common view of depressive disorders as predominantly having to do with mood — current research suggests that cognitions and affects are not discrete kinds of perception; rather
they are interactive and interwoven in experience. Attitudes
such as helplessness and hopelessness result from the combination of cognitions and affects the individual develops regarding the world and future events and can be important
components of an individual's psychological profile. Investigations of hopelessness, for example, suggest that it is a key
ingredient in adult suicide attempts (Beck, Kovacs, & Weissman, 1975). When Beck and his colleagues studied 384 suicide attempters (mean age 30 years) at two metropolitan
hospitals, they found that hopelessness was, in fact, a
stronger indicator of suicidal intent than depression.

One important area of investigation on the role of cognitions in psychopathology has focused on how the experience
of control (or lack of control) may render an individual more
or less susceptible to disorder. We have examined the development of the self as a function of the infant's expanding
regulatory system. Since self-regulation and self-control are

closely related (Trad, 1986, 1987), the characteristic ways in which the infant attempts to control itself and its environment *become* the infant. Indeed, from these modes of self-regulation and self-control originates a recognizable personality.

Traditional psychoanalytic theory has attached a great deal of importance to the individual's ability to control the self and the environment, as well as to the individual's perceptions of such control. The ability to modulate impulses and mediate their interactions with the environment is a hallmark of adaptive functioning (Trad, 1986, 1988). Psychological structures developed for this purpose are collectively known as ego. In attempting to operationalize the concept of adaptive ego functioning, Block and Block (J. Block, 1950; J. H. Block, 1951; J. H. Block & J. Block, 1980) describe the objectives of ego control as maximizing the expression of impulses while maintaining a tolerable level of anxiety and acceptably safe interactions with the environment. Ego control, as described by the Blocks, has much in common with the construct of temperament (Buss & Plomin, 1975; Rothbart & Derryberry, 1982; Thomas et al., 1968), in that both relate to individual differences in style of modulation or regulation of reactivity level. The temperamental dimensions of activity level, threshold, intensity, and distractibility (Thomas et al., 1968) describe the types of modulations accomplished by ego control.

When ego control fails, overcontrol or undercontrol tends to occur. Overcontrol implies containment of impulses and feelings, lack of responsiveness, inhibition of action, and delay of gratification. Undercontrol of the ego results in the immediate and direct expression of impulses and feelings, high levels of distractibility, unacceptable aggression, and lack of socialization. This dysregulation has been associated with disordered behavior (Trad, 1986, 1987). In a longitudinal study begun in 1968 that tracked children at ages three, four, five, seven, and eleven, Block and Block found that overcontrol and an inability to coordinate different control structures and to respond flexibly to environmental demands place a child at risk for psychopathology. The latter quality, which taps the adaptiveness of ego control, is called *ego brittleness* by the Blocks. In contrast to ego resilience, which implies fluid approaches to problem-solving, ego brittleness suggests a tendency toward disorganization in the face of altered circumstances and is reminiscent of Main's (Main, Kaplan, & Cassidy, 1985; Radke-Yarrow, Cummings, Kuczynski, & Chapman, 1985) description of "disorganized/ disoriented" infants. These infants have been shown to be at particularly high risk for depression. High ego resiliency, on the other hand, appears to correlate with positive patterns of social interaction.

Block and Block's concept of ego control is both broad and inclusive. The ego's efforts to exert control over the impulses clearly extend into several domains; also, the ego may function more successfully in one domain than in another. Consequently, while Block and Block's research helps validate previously unsubstantiated hypotheses concerning the importance of control in adaptation, it does not provide the specificity that would enable us to assess the contribution of various facets of ego functioning to the overall attainment of ego control. However, one facet of ego functioning – cognition – has been operationalized with respect to the development of control. On the pages that follow we will explore how cognitions related to control affect adaptation.

As is true of any belief system, beliefs about control may be realistic or unrealistic. Individuals with a strong perception of control are likely to attribute to themselves control over outcomes that are in fact not governable by personal actions. Individuals whose sense of control is less compelling tend to deny or fail to recognize the degree of control they actually possess in relation to a given end result.

Ironically, an unrealistic assumption about control may prove to be the most "rational" belief system to adopt in terms of achieving maximum adaptive functioning. For example, the optimal technique for developing a strong adaptive capacity may be to assume personal responsibility for successes but to attribute failures to forces over which the self has no control (e.g., bad luck). Since beliefs about control are related to self-esteem (the higher the degree of perceived control the greater the self-esteem), this defensive belief system enables the individual's self-perception to benefit maximally from success and suffer minimally from failure.

As assessment progresses, it will be useful to reach a conclusion about Lisa's attributional style; that is, does she attribute the outcome of events to her own actions or to outside forces? If her locus of control is even marginally more internal than external, it may be hypothesized that her current difficulties will subside following the initial trauma of separation from her mother, providing that Lisa's father is adequate to the task of fulfilling her needs.

THE DEVELOPMENT OF CONTROL

Q: When you go to bed, do you fall asleep right away?
A: Yes.
Q: How long do you practice the violin each day?
A: An hour.

Before assessing Lisa's beliefs about locus of control, it will be helpful to understand the dynamics underlying the development of assumptions about the way in which events are controlled. There are actually two types of control or mastery which confront the newborn infant: control of his/her own responses (both physical and affective) and control of the environment including, most critically, the caregiver. In order to control the environment, the infant must also learn to control itself. Crying in response to internally perceived stress leads to a response from the caregiver, a process which results in the perception of causality and development of the ability to at least partially self-regulate crying behavior. Thus, the infant comes to control the environment by controlling itself.

Self-control develops as a product of the interaction between growing abilities and growing awareness of the world and limitations on the controllability of that world. At birth, the human infant is endowed with a variety of perceptual and regulatory abilities. Regulatory abilities include the capacity to focus or avert attention and to adjust physical states (e.g., waking and sleeping) – two capacities which Lisa certainly possesses.

The neonate also has a repertoire of constitutionally determined responses which it uses to modulate both physiological and affective states. These traits are considered to exist along a continuum from extreme outgoingness to excessive withdrawal. Generally, those who are withdrawn are at greater risk for developing depressive-like phenomena (Trad, 1986, 1987). Therefore, since temperamental traits can be inherited to varying degrees, Lisa may have an extra measure of risk for developing depression, since both her parents appear to be more withdrawn than outgoing. Within the broad range of introverted-extroverted temperamental traits employed in the service of adaptive learning are individual differences in intensity, speed, regularity, and other qualities, such as the ability to shift into and out of different affective states.

To this fundamental repertoire of intrinsic responses are added voluntary (controlled) responses chosen as the infant interacts with the environment. The way in which the infant exercises the first rudiments of adaptive control and voluntary self-regulation is a function of the infant's ability to detect the difference between more and less pleasurable stimuli and to associate specific behaviors with their outcomes. Once an infant has developed the cognitive capacity to discriminate between stimuli with different degrees of appeal and to anticipate and perceive cause-and-effect relationships (i.e., primary circular reactions and contingency awareness), the infant may begin to establish its first perceptions about control.

One of the first steps in acquiring a "philosophy" of control, be it internal or external, is the gradual perception of discrepancies during dyadic interactions. Discrepancy awareness, in which the infant detects differences between various environmental stimuli, may exist as early as 28 hours after birth (Freedman, Carlsmith, & Sears, 1974). It appears that the differences – or discrepancies – between past and present stimuli have a greater effect on the infant's attention than the nature of any specific stimulus, and that moderate levels of discrepancy are the most stimulating (McCall & McGhee, 1977). These findings are logical enough, since any discrepancy within the otherwise homogeneous environment of the infant will probably be regarded as a potential threat that requires immediate attention. Moderate levels of discrepancy will be most stimulating because they will carry the possibility of control, thus being highly rewarding.

Closely following the developments of discrepancy awareness comes the formation of expectancies, which are internal models of the differences between various environmental stimuli (Mast, Fagen, Rovee-Collier, & Sullivan, 1980; Stern & Gibbon, 1978). With the formation of a workable set of expectancies, the young child can move on to develop an awareness of contingencies. Watson (1966) defines contingency perception as the ability to formulate specific strategies for achieving goals (control) by perceiving a cause and effect relation between two or more stimuli. With the development of an internal awareness of contingency, the child formally enters into the learning process – a process that hinges on the understanding of cause and effect (White, 1959).

The perception of contingency is associated from the earliest days of development with a powerful affective component (DeCasper & Carstens, 1981; Watson & Ramey, 1972). Contingency perception carries with it positive affect because it is invested with predictability, which carries the possibility of safety and control. The positive affective component also serves an adaptive function, stimulating the infant to exercise ever greater control over itself and the environment.

In terms of the development of contingency, Lisa may have been at a disadvantage, since episodes of separation are, in effect, massive breaks in the internal expectancy/contingency structure. Separation from the caregiver is perhaps the most traumatic experience a young child can endure. As such, great efforts are mobilized against it. In Lisa's case, however, these efforts have been of no avail. While separations certainly do not always result in permanent impairment of feelings about control, it is safe to say that for an infant or young child, such separations generally have a negative effect on the processes of cognitive and affective development.

Perhaps offsetting the negative influence of Lisa's experienced separations on her development of contingency is the fact that, for the infant, the primary focus of contingency learning and control is the caregiver. From the earliest moments of life, the caregiver is the most responsive element in the infant's environment. Watson (1966) interprets simple, repetitive, back-and-forth responses between caregiver and infant as the infant's experiments with contingency. By initiating an action such as a smile, the infant can create a similar response in the caregiver. This evokes positive feelings in the infant, which leads to further smiling, and so on, until the infant reaches its highest level of arousal and turns away. It may be argued that the motivating force in these interactions is the pleasure of creating a contingency. White (1959) calls this phenomenon "effectance pleasure," a pleasure which derives from exerting control over the environment.

It follows that the degree to which the caregiver is responsive to the infant's expression will determine the quality of the affect and will contribute in significant part to the infant's earliest sense of control. More immediate (and, to the infant, more contingent) responses on the part of the caregiver will engender greater feelings of efficacy in the infant. Unresponsiveness will be experienced with frustration and, eventually, a sense of helplessness. Since the infant cannot control everything in its environment, some degree of frustration is inevitable. The balance of success to frustration, or efficacy to helplessness will be a determining factor in the development of locus of control, self-esteem, and ultimately an integrated and stable self-concept.

With regard to the caregiver's role in helping the child

establish contingency awareness and, subsequently, an internal locus of control, Lisa's mother appears to have behaved (and continues to behave) in a consistent and loving manner. Despite her overall subdued demeanor, her affection for her daughter is apparent, and Lisa's return of that affection is guarded but heartfelt. Also, the fact that Lisa was separated from her parents at two and a half rather than at age two is probably fortunate. While it would have been better if Lisa had not suffered feelings of abandonment at any point in her short life, she was probably better able to cope with those feelings once the crucial separation-individuation process was well underway – a process that begins at around 18 months of age. From the age of one and a half to two and a half, Lisa continued to experience a secure relationship with her mother, living at home with a trusted nanny while she fought to establish her independent being and to work out a system of self-object differentiation (the object being primarily her mother). Thus, she had one year to establish herself as somewhat independent from her mother before her mother departed for Europe. The trauma would have been much greater had the separation occurred earlier, when Lisa's sense of self was still inextricably linked to her mother. Given Lisa's outstanding achievements for her age, it would seem she made good use of whatever degree of contingency there was in her environment and of the opportunity to differentiate from her mother on a secure basis. With regard to her evident sadness, one must not forget that she is confronting the prospect of imminent separation while struggling to meet her parents' high expectations for her.

CONTROL THEORIES

Q: When you really, truly want something, do you think you
     usually get it?
A: (smiling) Oh, sure!

Theories of control are rooted in the idea that some events are controllable by voluntary action and some are not, and that a person can learn which is true for a given event. When we speak of control in these terms, we are speaking of control over the environment rather than of control of the self. Voluntary responses, the concern of control theory, differ from involuntary or reflex responses in that voluntary responses can be modified by reward or punishment. Voluntary responses change in relation to the contingency or outcome. If a person is given ten dollars every time he reads a newspaper, he is more likely to read the newspaper daily – or even several times a day. This is a voluntary response. Involuntary responses, such as the contraction of the pupil when exposed to a bright light, will not change whether the person is rewarded or punished as a result. The study of operant conditioning, upon which the learned helplessness model is based, is concerned with voluntary response.

In order to determine whether an event is controllable, a person must decide whether the event is *response dependent* or *response independent*. This kind of learning occurs in several ways. The most basic is the direct connection of a voluntary response with an outcome. This is called *continuous reinforcement*. For example, an infant in a playground raises his arm to wave at his mother. Every time he does so, the mother smiles and waves back. In this fashion, the behavior is reinforced. If the infant waves, but the mother is busy talking to a neighbor and does not wave back, the response will not be followed by the desired outcome. If this happens several times, the infant will quit trying; the result is *extinction*. If the mother's attention is never on the infant and she never waves back, the infant will conclude that nothing can be done to produce the desired outcome – i.e., the event is uncontrollable – and he will eventually cease to wave at her. He may eventually experience negative affect associated with the mother. In this case, while Lisa may feel some reservation, or even ambivalence, about her mother, it seems doubtful that she suffered truly high levels of maternal noncontingency as an infant. Had her mother been nonresponsive to a high degree, it is unlikely that Lisa would have attained the level of adaptive functioning she now displays.

Other than continuous reinforcement or extinction, there is also the possibility of *partial* or *intermittent reinforcement*. An infant may find that his mother waves back sometimes, fails to wave sometimes, and sometimes waves without his waving first. In other words, his response is reinforced partially and intermittently. If there is a preponderance of one contingency, the infant will make a determination that the event is more or less response dependent. If the infant decides that the event is equally likely to occur in the presence or absence of the response, he will decide that the event is response independent. Thus, the infant might eventually come to decide that waving had no effect on whether or not the mother waved back. Skinner (1969) found partial reinforcement to be more resistant to extinction than continuous reinforcement. That is, if mother sometimes waves back and then ceases to wave completely, the infant will try to elicit a response from her by waving longer than if mother had begun by responding to every wave (continuous reinforcement) and had then ceased.

It is important to note that a controllable response need not be a desired response. If a person finds that a particular behavior increases the likelihood of *not* getting a desired response, then that outcome is controllable by not using that behavior. If the infant finds that whenever he waves and yells, the mother turns away and talks to her neighbor, he will decide that his attempts to induce the mother to wave are negatively associated with the desired outcome. Only outcomes which are totally noncontingent are uncontrollable.

Additions to learning theory that take into account the role of self-awareness in the impact of reinforcement and reward became prominent in the literature in the middle 1960s. (Rotter, 1966; Seligman & Maier, 1967; Watson, 1966). The result was that the model of operant conditioning, as applied to humans, had to be expanded to include not only the effect of reward and punishment, but also the perception of the relation between reinforcement and the behavior that was being reinforced. Briefly, if the child receives a reward associated with a specific outcome, the behavior will be reinforced only if the child can perceive a relationship between it and the outcome. Since individuals can perceive outcomes as being contingent on forces outside themselves, reinforcement will only produce an increase in a specific activity if the reward is perceived as being contingent on the individual's behavior. Conversely, if an individual becomes convinced that aversive stimuli are not contingent on any actions within his or her control, the individual will cease to attempt to escape the stimuli.

Rotter (1966) has emphasized the importance of the perception of contingency in determining the effects of reinforcement. An event that is perceived as being contingent upon the individual's behavior is termed "internally controlled." If an event is perceived as being not contingent on the individual's behavior, it may be perceived as being contingent upon luck, chance, fate, powerful others, or it may be viewed as being unpredictable due to a combination of determining factors. All of these attributions come under the heading of "external control."

Since contingencies strengthen the expectancy that a specific behavior will result in a predictable outcome, Rotter theorized that individuals' previous experience of contingency would cause them to show individual differences in a generalized tendency to attribute events to their own actions. Individuals who generally adopt the outlook that contingencies are within their control are said to have an "internal locus of control." Those who consistently view outcomes as being determined by forces outside of or beyond themselves are described as having an "external locus of control."

Rotter's (1966) "I-E Scale" has been widely used for measuring individual's locus of control orientation. It consists of 30 pairs of statements. Respondents are asked to select which statement in each pair best reflects their attitude. One statement in each pair betrays an external locus of control and the other an internal orientation. For example, in the pair of statements on the subject of government, the statement, "The average citizen can have an influence in government decisions," shows more of an internal orientation than the statement, "This world is run by the few people in power, and there is not much the little guy can do about it."

There is, nevertheless, still some confusion about what constitutes internality and externality. Rotter (1966) defines internality in terms of self-causality and self-contingency. However, Rothbaum, et al., (1982) criticize this definition as incomplete, maintaining that one must take into account the subject's assessment of his or her abilities. Feelings that an event is uncontrollable due to lack of ability imply a lack of contingency between the self and the environment but are still self-attributed. The self is blamed for its inability to control the outcome.

However, the individual does not easily accept the notion of uncontrollable outcomes. For example, Brehm (1966) has developed a reactance theory focusing on the relationship between specific behavioral outcomes and perceptions about control. This theory suggests that threats to an individual's freedom to engage in or control a specific behavior will lead to increasing efforts to engage in that behavior and possibly to hostile and aggressive manifestations in this effort. This theory may, to some degree, account for Lisa's problematic behavior in school. It seems plausible that, given her high achievement level in reading and music, her parents may have frustrated her early attempts at playing in favor of more disciplined pursuits. Now that she is in an environment where such play behavior is allowed, Lisa literally may be going at it with a vengeance.

This possibility gains credence from the fact that much of Seligman's (e.g., 1975) early work with dogs subjected to uncontrollability (i.e., learned helplessness) has been observed to be applicable to humans. Dogs and humans alike exhibit cognitive, emotional, and motivational deficits when subjected to uncontrollable stress. Researchers examining specific aspects of intellectual and emotional functioning, as well as broader measures of perceived competence, have amassed virtually incontrovertible evidence of the far-reaching impact of the individual's control beliefs on the individual's adaptive functioning.

THE DYNAMICS OF LEARNING TO ADAPT

Q: If you could choose between playing the violin for your parents or playing with your friends, which would you like better?
A: Playing the violin.
Q: Why do you like the violin better?
A: (Lisa answers precisely) 'Cause mommy likes me to play and 'cause I can be alone.

Once contingency awareness triggers the development of an orientation about locus of control, the process of adaptation to the environment begins in earnest. Given that the desire for control is a primary motivator of adaptive behavior, assessing the level of adaptive learning provides another means of measuring the child's locus of control. For example, a high level of adaptive learning would suggest that the child strongly believes it is possible to achieve a good deal of control over the environment. Thus, if adaptive behavior is "average or above," the likelihood that the child has an internal versus an external LOC is increased. When examining Lisa's level of adaptation as an index of LOC, it is important to keep in mind that academic and musical achievement are by no means sufficient criteria for measuring the ability to cope or adapt.

Rothbaum, et al., (1982) argue that adaptive control involves two processes: bringing the environment into accord and equilibrium with the individual and bringing the individual into accord and equilibrium with the environment. Adaptation, therefore, should be defined as knowledge of how and when it is necessary to employ each form of control. Children who fail to gain a sense of control over their emotions and impulses may be as much at risk for psychopathology as those who do not experience a feeling of control over their environment. Hyperactive children, for example, have been shown to differ from nonhyperactive children in how much subjective control they experience (Linn & Hodge, 1982). While Lisa might, under some circumstances, appear to be somewhat hyperactive, her behavior is generally too controlled to warrant the label of hyperactivity – a good sign in terms of locus of control. However, her preference for the solitary activity of playing the violin may indicate a certain degree of discomfort with internal emotions, since social situations have a greater potential to bring out emotionality.

Different evaluations about one's degree of control over the environment have been observed to be associated with distinct coping styles, and this, too, might be of value in assessing Lisa's risk of psychopathology. Although Davidson (1975) questions the discriminating validity of some control theories, numerous studies have documented a less effective coping style among those who perceive themselves as lacking control over the environment.

Studying the behavior of British nurses, Parkes (1984) found that in clear-cut stressful situations, the coping style of those with a greater sense of internal control was more focused than that of those with a lesser sense of control. (A clear-cut stressful situation was defined as one in which the respondent thought she could either change the situation or had to accept it.) In more ambiguous situations – those where the respondent felt she required more information in order to act or had to hold back from doing something she wanted to do – Parkes found that those with a strong sense of control adopt a more general coping strategy which differs from that employed by those with a lesser sense of control.

Parkes also observed completely opposite coping patterns between the two groups when a situation was judged as being amenable to change. Those with a strong sense of inner control demonstrated a significantly greater tendency than the latter to use rational task-oriented coping strategies. They were also less likely than those with a weaker sense of control to suppress thoughts and feelings about internal LOC and displayed a more flexible coping style, while their counterparts responded more rigidly, altering

their coping behaviors very little in relation to their appraisal of the situation.

Many of the original investigations of control theories
used adult subjects and established clear patterns of association between specific cognitions related to control and
broad levels of competence. Indeed, efforts to tap broad levels of competence as a function of control beliefs have yield-
ed remarkably consistent results. For example, Seeman and
Evans (1962) found that patients who were more internally
controlled knew more about their condition, questioned their
doctors and nurses more and expressed less satisfaction
with the treatment they were getting. The researchers interpreted this to mean that people with a greater sense of control tend to exert a greater effort to improve their circumstances. The researchers noticed that the greater the sense
that events were controlled by forces other than the self, the
greater the emergence of feelings of powerlessness.

Perceptions related to control have an effect on the kind of
coping strategies used to manage stress. Some researchers
have found that those with a strong sense of control experience less distress and achieve better outcomes in response
to serious stressors (Anderson, 1977). Anderson (1977) has
demonstrated that those with a strong sense of control consistently use coping strategies different from those used by
people lacking such a sense of control. Specifically, they employed more task-oriented and less emotionally-oriented behaviors. Parkes (1984) notes that such individuals tend to
use coping strategies which focus on altering a stressful situation, whereas those without a strong sense of control tend
to employ strategies designed to alter the perception of the
situation into a nonthreatening one. In determining the type
of coping strategy selected, perception of a situation had a
strong effect on those with a strong sense of control. Faced
with situations that they perceived were within their power
to change, they assessed the needs of the situation more
accurately than did those with less robust feelings of control,
and consequently responded with fewer and more appropriate strategies.

In her analysis, Parkes separated coping strategies into "direct coping" and "suppression." Direct coping included attempts to alter a stressful situation either through individual action or by enlisting the aid of others, as well as expressions of hostility and fantasy. Suppression describes attempts to avoid thoughts and feelings about the stressful situation. In measurements of direct coping versus suppression, Parkes found that those with a strong sense of control favored direct coping in relation to the degree to which they interpreted the situation as amenable to change. Conversely, in situations perceived as amenable to change, those without a strong sense of control showed higher levels of suppression versus direct coping. For both, the inability to suppress stressful reactions is a hallmark of episodes that are perceived as highly important.

In nonsocial test situations, Lisa demonstrated predominantly flexible strategies in solving problems, suggesting an internal locus of control. However, in circumstances in which she was involved with other children of her age in a problem-solving task, Lisa sometimes demonstrated an unfocused approach, leaving the solving to others or only occasionally making a half-hearted suggestion. These observations suggest that while Lisa may have good control of the environment (as evidenced by her advanced achievements and performance on tests), she may not have an equal command of her internal self, e.g., impulse control and the ability to modulate herself adaptively from moment to moment in response to the behavior of those around her. Since those who have a poor sense of internal control are as much at risk as those who poorly control the environment, Lisa may be at some risk for psychopathology in this regard.

INTERACTION BETWEEN CONTROL AND DEPRESSION

Q: How do you feel when it takes a long time to learn a new song on the violin?

A: I hate it! I get mad when I can't make my fingers work fast enough.
Q: Does it make you cry when you can't learn a song?
A: Sometimes I cry.
Q: You cry because you're mad?
A: Because I can't do it (her face clouds). I'm stupid.

Now that we have explored the nature and development of an individual's locus of control, it is time to focus more closely on Lisa's risk of developing depression by examining the relationship between control and depression. As we can see from Lisa's feelings while learning a difficult piece of music, an inability to achieve control according to self-expectations can easily lead to decrements in self-esteem, a mechanism that can quickly give rise to depression. A vast amount of theoretical and empirical work has concerned itself with the depressive impact of certain control beliefs.

The theoretical relationship between depression and perceptions of uncontrollability is most clearly delineated by the learned helplessness model, in both its original and reformulated forms (Abramson, et al., 1978; Peterson & Seligman, 1984; Seligman, 1975; Seligman & Maier, 1967). The central prediction of this model is that repeated exposure to uncontrollable events creates an expectation of future uncontrollability that results in a dysregulation of behavior and subsequent feelings of debilitating hopelessness.

The dysregulation occurs in the form of four deficits — motivational, cognitive, affective, and self-esteem — all of which may find expression in depressed symptomatology. Indeed, the picture of lowered affect and hopelessness created by learned helplessness so closely parallels the classic picture of depression that the process by which this develops is easily taken as a metaphor for the kind of catastrophic personal events that lead to reactive depressions. Seligman (1975) describes six symptoms of learned helplessness (LH) that have direct parallels in depression:

1) lowered initiation of voluntary response;
2) negative cognitive set;

3) time course—both helplessness and depression fade away following a single initial shock, but after repeated shocks, both persist;
4) loss of appetite—helpless individuals eat less, have lowered sexual desires and lowered social abilities;
5) physiological changes—changes in neurochemicals such as norepinephrine and cortisol are associated with depression.

Although the learned helplessness theory emphasizes the cognitive attributions of depression, Seligman is quick to point out that the separation of cognition and affect is a descriptive dichotomy and not one that exists in the individual, where thoughts and feelings are experienced as indistinguishably intermixed.

The causes of learned helplessness and some depressions are similar in that they both emphasize uncontrollability. Traumatic events such as the death of a loved one—or, as in Lisa's case, separation from loved ones—divorce, loss of job, old age, and illness all share the quality of being beyond the individual's personal control. These are the kind of events associated with reactive depression. When several of these occur within close temporal proximity, life's problems may seem insurmountable—i.e., the sufferer feels helpless—and depression can be severe. Seligman (1975) points out that there are individual (temperamental) differences in the degree to which people react to traumatic events with helplessness. In fact, he proposes that a propensity or predisposition to helplessness may be at the root of endogenous depression. By this measure, Lisa may be at risk if she shares her parents' basic internality. After several encounters with Lisa, this clinician did not detect this characteristic in her; rather, she was uniformly outgoing.

Cognitions surrounding the issue of control (i.e., the expectation of future uncontrollability) not only act to predict the existence of depression, but also foreshadow its chronicity and severity. These issues are taken up by the theory's reformulations (Abramson, et al., 1978). The reformulation focuses not on the expectation of future uncontrollability but on the individual's explanation for the original bad events. According to the reformulated helplessness model, individuals whose explanatory style leads them to cite internal, stable, and global causes for the negative events they encounter tend to be at risk for depression.

These qualities – internality, stability, and globality – lie at the end of three dimensions related to the attribution of helplessness. For descriptive purposes, these dimensions are represented as dichotomies, but the theorists point out that these dichotomies are actually the end points along an attributional continuum.

(1) Universal vs. Personal Helplessness

If a person believes that another person in a relevant peer group would also be helpless in the same situation, then the helplessness is considered to be universal. On the other hand, if the individual believes that another person would not be helpless in the same situation, then the helplessness is interpreted to be personal in origin. In this model, personal helplessness, in which the negative outcome is perceived as contingent on internal factors, is experienced with negative self-esteem. Universal helplessness, wherein bad events are attributed to external factors, do not imply an internal failure and therefore are not accompanied by feelings of loss of self-esteem, In this regard, we have seen that Lisa probably experiences loss of self-esteem in social problem-solving situations, which adds to her risk for depression.

(2) Stable vs. Unstable

Those events which are attributed to stable factors are more likely to generalize to other situations. For example, a person who attributes failure to an innate lack of ability is likely to perceive his or her helplessness as internal and stable. Failure that is attributed to lack of effort is seen as correctable. This kind of attribution is internal and unstable. Failure perceived as due to the difficulty of a task would be external and stable (here Lisa performs well, being able to accurately discriminate relative task difficulties). Failure perceived as being attributable to lack of luck would be external and unstable and would not be likely to generalize to any other trials. In short, the reformulated helplessness theory suggests that helplessness will persist until the attribution can be shifted to an unstable element.

Although the determination of whether a particular cause is stable or unstable is highly subjective (Trad, 1987, 1988), causes such as task difficulty are commonly assumed to be on the stable end of the spectrum and causes such as effort and luck are usually thought of as examples of unstable causes. Thus, expectancies change more when attributed to stable causes than to unstable causes. The expectancy of success will increase more after a successful trial, and decrease more after a failure, if the success is attributed to ability rather than to luck.

With the foregoing in mind, it would seem advisable to place Lisa in as many social problem-solving situations as possible, praising her for all successful outcomes. In this way, with the help of her parents (or, in the absence of her mother, her father), Lisa might come to believe more strongly in the contingency of her actions and positive outcomes, decreasing any valency there might be toward depression and helplessness.

(3) Global vs. Specific

Global attributions are those which affect a wide variety of outcomes. A student who fails a math test may attribute his or her failure to an inability in math or to an inability to take tests in general. The more global attribution may generalize helplessness to other situations. Thus, it will be important to discourage Lisa from engaging in global attributions for negative outcomes.

The investigators further suggest that the intensity of

motivational and cognitive deficits is related to the strength and certainty of the expectation of noncontingency. The intensity of affective and self-esteem deficits is related to the certainty and importance of the event which is uncontrollable. A sad or depressive affect is found only when the uncontrollable outcome is an undesired one. Uncontrollable positive events cause cognitive and motivational deficits without sad affect.

Justifications for using these qualities to evaluate a child as young as Lisa, focusing on her propensity for depression and its currently experienced intensity, come from many sources in the literature. These support the applicability of the learned helplessness model to children. Seligman and Peterson (1986; Seligman, Kaslow, Alloy, Peterson, Tannenbaum, & Abramson, 1984) conducted a series of tests in children between the ages of eight and twelve and found that children undergo the same deficits of cognition, motivation, and affect that are associated with learned helplessness in adults. They further found that attributional style is a risk factor for depression in children, just as it is in adults.

Furthermore, the literature on self-esteem provides strong support for the proposition that children's beliefs about their ability to control the environment have a profound impact on their self-esteem, thereby affecting their risk for developing depression. A study by Zautra, et al., (1985) confirmed findings that associated internal attributions for positive events with high self-esteem. Conversely, internal stable attributions for negative events were associated with depression. Unstable attributions showed no correlation with depression.

Additionally, in a longitudinal study by Jones (1978) locus of control among fourth and fifth graders related strongly to their self-concept. In a related investigation dealing with children of roughly Lisa's age onward, Prawat, Grissom, and Parish (1979) found a high correlation between self-esteem and locus of control in children in elementary, junior high, and high school.

CONTROL AND MOTIVATION

Q: Do you ever feel like giving up when you can't learn a new
  piece of music?
A: I can't. Mommy won't let me.

Just as control and depression are related, so too are control and motivational level. Learned helplessness theory predicts that motivational deficits will accompany the cognitive and emotional deficits produced by repeated exposure to uncontrollability. Such motivational deficits were initially observed among dogs who made few attempts to escape the uncontrollable electrical shocks to which they had been exposed. Learned helplessness theorists interpreted this seemingly helpless behavior as evidence that the dogs had developed the expectation of future noncontingency between response and outcome.

The effects of a perception of uncontrollability appeared to reverberate through many areas of the dogs' emotional and cognitive functioning. Since the motive to achieve success leads to creative, exploratory behavior and the motive to avoid failure provokes inhibitory responses, it is not surprising that a perception of helplessness can stifle learning motivation. While Lisa remains well motivated to achieve success, her response to my inquiry about giving up indicates that she does experience some feelings of helplessness, since she sees the reason for her efforts as originating outside of herself. In other words, she is demonstrating an urge to avoid failure, rather than achieve success. Numerous researchers (Brophy & Good, 1974; Crandall, 1967; Licht & Dweck, 1981; Nicholls, 1981; Wine, 1982) have demonstrated the significant effect of motivation on children's intellectual performance.

Anticipating a valued outcome aids in the initiation of a task and persistence in it (Schunk, 1983). Wolf and Savickas (1985) referred to an "integrated time perspective" and hypothesized that it would correlate with internal attributions for success and external attributions for failure – internal causes being associated with optimism. They also hypothesized that a time perspective would not relate to stability or instability of causes. The subjects in the study by Wolf and Savickas were tenth graders in a middle-class suburb with an average age of 16 years. The results confirmed the correlation between an integrated time perspective and internal attributions for success and external attributions for failures. This set of attributions enhances self-esteem both by associating success with internal factors and by protecting against negative self-attributions.

The study of motivation examines choices made about goal-directed activity and includes an examination of children's assessments of task difficulty and personal abilities, inferences made concerning task outcomes, valuations of the worth of projected goals, problem-solving strategies, and performance monitoring. In making assessments about goal-directed activity, children are, to a large extent, making decisions about the amount of control they can exert over their environment. The expectancies revolving around the relationship between future responses and future outcomes—in other words, expectancies about control—are clearly operating beneath any determination of one's ability to achieve specified goals.

Need achievement theory (Atkinson, 1964; McClelland, Atkinson, Clark & Lowell, 1953), which describes motivation in terms of the motive to achieve success and the motive to avoid failure, underscores the importance of the anticipatory effect of the outcome on motivation. Donaldson (1978) and Harter (1981) describe mastery motivation as a basic urge to manage the environment. Dweck and Elliot (1983) refer to achievement motivation, which differs from mastery motivation in that it includes goals related to self-efficacy (task mastery) and goals related to external evaluations. White (1959) felt that effectance pleasure, the positive affect associated with the creation of contingent events, represents a kind of motivation. He felt that such effectance pleasure propels children toward learning and is the basis of positive self-esteem.

Thus, some of the mechanisms that shape expectancies about control should also influence motivation. Conditions that create negative expectations of future response-outcome dependence should be expected to interfere with motivation. However, the investigations of Slade, Steward, Morrison, and Abramowitz (1984) have raised questions about how motivation is influenced by contingency information received by children. Somewhat surprisingly, these researchers found that abused children, whose overall attributional style was more external than that of the nonabused children studied, displayed comparable levels of persistence in the face of repeated noncontingent failure. A persistence task with a high failure rate, administered in an unfamiliar setting, did not appear to elicit more defeatism or incompetence among abused than among nonabused children.

One explanation for this surprising finding may be the methodology used, as the authors acknowledge. Another reason, however, may lie in the contention of some that cognitions are only one influence on the expectancies that underlie motivation. For example, Piaget (1925, 1929) has suggested that children tend to form expectations based on their desires. The empirical work of Stipek, Roberts, and Sanborn (1984) has borne this out. In researching the expectations of task-related success that four-year-olds had for themselves and others, the investigators found that young children possess the cognitive skills to make predictions based on past contingencies, but that they frequently fail to distinguish between their desires and their expectations. They also found that, while these children commonly did not take into account past performance in predicting success for themselves, they were able to do so in predicting other four-year-olds' performance. Salient evidence of their past performance record was needed for them to make realistic predictions for themselves.

Although the varieties of attributional style are responsible for many kinds of cognitive and affective distortions, all forms of attribution have an impact on motivation and serve some adaptive function. Control is always preferred over lack of control, and the experience of noncontingent events leads to various defensive strategies that seek to maintain an acceptable level of apparent control.

Studies of learned helplessness usually show subjects reacting with lowered motivation and lessened response, in order to conserve energy in a situation where no response is perceived as effective. These responses have often been interpreted as abandonment of the effort for control. Rothbaum, Weisz, and Snyder (1982), on the other hand, contend that the motivation for control is rarely abandoned and what the behaviors control theorists interpret as resignation actually reflect a different kind of effort to maintain control. They propose that the "inward" behaviors that control theorists observe among those thought to relinquish control be interpreted as adaptive attempts to maintain control in situations of apparent uncontrollability. They refer to these efforts as attempts to achieve "secondary control"—to manipulate perceptions to match the demands of the environment—in contrast to "primary control" in which an individual attempts to manipulate the environment. Included in secondary control are attempts to give meaning to uncontrollable events through lowered expectations or identification with chance or other powerful agents. The researchers note that in practice primary control and secondary control mix; in the real world, almost all attempts to manipulate the environment involve some element of compromise and change in outlook.

The researchers feel that an important element in perception of control is the fulfillment of expectations. The ability to predict outcomes, even negative outcomes, is one type of control and is preferable to inability to predict. Individuals who experience repeated failures may come to approach a task with minimal effort, even when they have a good chance of succeeding. In this way, they guard against disappointment and gain a measure of control over a potentially negative situation. Attributions to limited ability (e.g., "I'm never good at this kind of test") are interpreted as a means of lowering expectations. "Predictive control" is the name the

researchers give to this type of attribution. It is important
to note that according to Rothbaum, Weisz, and Snyder, predictability is more important in these situations than the
possible self-esteem which might accrue from a success. Another interpretation is that, after the experience of a series of
failures, a single success is perceived as the result of chance
and has less positive effect on self-esteem than does the ability to predict the next outcome.

Predictability is perceived as a positive attribute to
events, and the lack of predictability is avoided. Controversy
has arisen over the last 20 years, as various investigators
have attempted to explain the effects of controllability in
terms of predictability and vice versa. Some research has
shown that the *expectation* of control can have the same
effects on motivation as actual control over events (Gatchel,
1980; Miller, 1979). Mineka and Hendersen's (1985) review of
the literature on the interrelationship of predictability and
controllability concluded that the qualities of predictability
and controllability are interactive in their effects on the motivation, organization, and operation of behavior.

In terms of motivation, Lisa seems to come off rather well
in both the areas of desire for internal and external control.
This is a positive sign for internal LOC and for her ability to
avoid depression, although she does experience an imbalance
between control of the external and internal milieu.

CONTROL AND ANXIETY

Q: You are being very gentle to her (the female doll). Is she
   scared?
A: She's worried she'll be alone.
Q: Is there some reason she might be alone?
A: She just worries. I have to be nice to her.
Q: Why?
A: (angrily) Because she's scared! And she can't get away!

Anxiety symptoms appear commonly among those without a sense of control over their environment. Ollendick's
(1979) study of 134 fourth graders of lower socioeconomic

status found that for both boys and girls higher trait anxiety correlated significantly with an external locus of control. Locus of control also appeared to have a predictable impact on children's locus of conflict. External LOC children reacted with behaviors, including hyperactivity, aggression and conduct disorders, reflecting a tendency to externalize (rather than internalize) conflict. Such externalization of conflict should be viewed with great concern in light of some evidence that externalizing behaviors show greater stability than internalizing behaviors (Fischer, Rolf, Hasazi, & Cummings, 1984).

Anxiety among adults also appears to correlate strongly with an external locus of control. Johnson and Sarason (1978) studied, among other phenomena, the effects of locus of control on trait and state anxiety among college students at the University of Washington. They observed that, when students were confronted with negative life events, those with external locus of control displayed higher levels of depression and trait anxiety than those with internal locus of control. When positive events occurred, however, locus of control did not offer comparable discriminating power. These observations led the researchers to conclude that a sense of control is important in moderating the effects of stress. Thus, externals who confront high levels of life stress should be considered at risk for psychiatric symptoms.

Lisa's noticeable anxiety is probably largely attributable to the impending departure of her mother, an external event she desperately wants to influence in her own favor but cannot. This anxiety, while it is unlikely to disappear altogether, will very likely diminish after she adjusts to her mother's absence and gains comfort from her father and from her own considerable ability to control other elements of her environment.

CONTROL AND AGGRESSION

Q: Did you ever hit anyone without being hit first?
A: I hit Barbara.

Q: Why did you hit her if she didn't hit you first?
A: She was playing my violin.
Q: Does she know how to play?
A: She takes lessons with me, but I don't let her use my violin!

Reactance theory (Brehm, 1966; Rothbaum, 1980), which can be viewed as a model parallel to learned helplessness, posits a relationship between reactive-aggressive (outward) behavior and uncontrollability. This theory suggests – and we see from the conversation above with Lisa – that when an individual's control of a specific behavior is threatened, the individual will increase his or her efforts to engage in that particular behavior and may exhibit hostile-aggressive behaviors in this effort. This "reactance" is the opposite of helpless behavior. Indeed, Ellis and Milner (1981) have shown that adults at risk for aggression – in the form of child abuse – are significantly more external than those not at risk.

Several researchers have attempted to develop a helplessness-reactance model including both responses. Rothbaum (1980) posits that individuals perceive different levels of uncontrollability. Low levels of uncontrollability, according to the researcher, lead to reactance. Higher levels of perceived uncontrollability lead to helplessness. Roth & Kubal (1975) and Tennen & Eller (1977) conducted experiments in which adult subjects were first exposed to a series of unsolvable problems, and then were administered a solvable task. Subjects who were exposed to a smaller number of unsolvable tasks demonstrated increased persistence in solving the later task, while subjects exposed to a greater number of unsolvable trials showed decreased persistence, i.e., helplessness. The researchers also found that the lesser degrees of uncontrollability (which led to increased persistence) were associated with feelings of anger, while the affective counterparts to lowered persistence were feelings of helplessness and incompetence.

These findings are easily explained by an operant conditioning approach to helplessness theory. Reactive behavior in the face of uncontrollability indicates that the subject has not received sufficient reinforcement to "learn" helplessness. Rothbaum (1980) points out that subjects will differ, according to their expectations of control, in the amount of reinforcement required to accept that they are helpless. If there is a contrast between expectations of control and subsequent perceptions of uncontrollability, the situation will be perceived as "loss of control" and be met with reactant behavior. If there is no expectation of control, uncontrollability will be perceived as "lack of control."

Rothbaum points out the pertinence of these distinctions to an understanding of the feeling of loss. Bowlby (1960, 1969, 1982) describes the progressive stages of reaction to the loss of a caregiver as "protest, despair, detachment." Protest behavior is manifested in reactive, violent attempts to regain the caregiver in his or her absence. After a prolonged period of failure at these attempts, the child enters a period of apathetic despair. This may be interpreted as a change from the perception of loss of control (over the caregiver) to a perception of lack of control. The child has learned that it is helpless to retrieve the caregiver; consequently it ceases to protest.

Rothbaum also points out that the perception of lack of control can also change to a perception of loss of control, with a resulting affective move from apathy to anger. He draws an analogy to the events which commonly precede a political revolution, in which a subservient class experiences a period of rising expectations and responds with aggressive rebellion. The perception of the impossibility of control has changed to a perception that control is possible but is being withheld.

Although Lisa is behaving aggressively at school, it is unlikely that this behavior stems from any sudden shift in her global feelings about control. The fact that aggressive behavior serves an adaptive learning function for children her age, together with the impending frustrating departure of her mother, provides an adequate explanation for her behavior. However, it is also possible that Lisa feels she might be able to control her mother's behavior, i.e., make her stay home, by the concern she demonstrates each time Lisa misbehaves in an aggressive fashion.

CONTROL AND HYPERACTIVITY

Q: What kinds of things do you like to do in school? Things that you have to sit down for or things where you stand up and move around?

A: Move!

Q: OK, but when you do have to sit down for awhile, is it hard?

A: No. If it's not too long.

Q: What's too long?

A: Like when we listen to Mrs. Madden (her preschool teacher) read to us (about 20 minutes).

Research on hyperactive children performed by Linn and Hodge (1982) reveals that the control construct can be used meaningfully to differentiate between hyperactive and nonhyperactive children. The 16 hyperactive children studied (mean age 6.3 years) were significantly more external than the 16 control children. Moreover, this investigation suggests that the interaction between mental age and locus of control orientation may differ over time between hyperactive and nonhyperactive children. It appears from this study that with increasing mental age nonhyperactive children grow progressively more internal. Among hyperactive children, however, greater mental age did not correlate with greater internality. The pronounced externality displayed by hyperactive children raises important therapeutic questions concerning the use of exclusively pharmacological treatments, which, as Linn and Hodge speculate, may reinforce hyperactive children's externality. Since Lisa, judging from her ability to sit and listen and to study, does not appear to be hyperactive, and her internality is likely to increase, there is little reason to be concerned for her in this regard.

CONTROL AND INTELLECTUAL DEVELOPMENT

Q: Do you like to read?
A: (emphatically) Oh, yes!
Q: Do you remember what you read?
A: Oh sure!
Q: Everything?
A: Most everything.

Numerous studies have correlated the development of control with intellectual development, with most investigations revealing that a strong sense of internal control is associated with greater intellectual development. Only a few studies—for example, those performed by Tolor, Tolor, and Blumin (1977) and Bladow (1982)—have failed to find a link between control beliefs and measures of intellectual development in young children. Most other studies have demonstrated that internality appears to promote intellectual development while externality appears to impede it. Lisa's accomplishments in reading and playing the violin argue strongly for a significant degree of healthy internality.

Studies of children with learning difficulties have helped to highlight the role of explanatory style in intellectual achievement. A review of the literature on locus of control and learning disabilities conducted by Dudley-Marling, Snider, and Tarver (1982) supports this view. Moreover, the specific pattern of locus of control orientation observed among learning-disabled children resembles learned helplessness, with external attributions for success and internal attributions for failure. This is not surprising given the frequent concurrence of learning disability and depression (Trad, 1987).

Other studies of learning-disabled children also indicate a strong relationship between learning disability and locus of control. Rogers and Saklofske (1985) studied locus of control beliefs, performance expectations, and self-concepts among seven-to-twelve year olds and found learning-disabled children were significantly more external than normal achievers. Moreover, the learning-disabled children had significantly lower self-concepts. Although the study did not specifically examine the success-failure dichotomy and locus of control beliefs of the children, the authors did suggest that differences will exist among the learning-disabled. Some may adopt a defensive attributional style and project blame for inadequacies on the environment, while others are more self-blaming. In both cases, however, understanding a child's locus of control orientation can help in predicting the potential manifestations of disorder and in devising appropriate treatment.

In a longitudinal study that evaluated subjects at 18 months, two years, and again at four to five years, Arend, et al., (1979) found a strong relationship between ego resilience and curiosity. Studies measuring academic achievement have also highlighted the contribution of explanatory style to intellectual development. At least one investigation of the effect of locus of control on academic achievement (Findley & Cooper, 1983) shows a small but definite relationship between internality and academic achievement. These researchers found the correlation greater in adolescents than in adults and greater in men than in women. They also found that the correlation was greater in controlled situations such as standardized tests than in classroom situations.

Younger children's locus of control orientation also appears to affect academic achievement. Swanson (1981), in a study of 48 learning-disabled boys (mean age 8.11 years), found that internal locus of control fostered higher achievement. Moreover, the study found external boys less able to withstand the impact of extended failure. Among external boys such failure led to significant declines in performance.

A larger study (452 boys and 492 girls with a mean age of 10.24) of academic achievement and locus of control revealed a strong correlation between external locus of control and lower academic achievement (Tesiny, et al., 1980). Furthermore, this study, which measured school achievement using teacher ratings as well as standardized math and reading scores, found that, although there was a significant relationship between externality and depression, the relationship

between externality and lowered achievement was more robust than that between externality and depression.

Using the single measurement of intellectual achievement, Lisa comes off very well in terms of having a solidly
based internal locus of control. Her musical and school abilities demonstrate a high degree of faith in herself, as well as a
good ability to regulate her impulses at a very young age.
However, working against her capacity to self-regulate her
behavior are possibly angry feelings arising from the perception that she is being pressured to achieve in order to "earn"
parental love. Such anger, if it exists, will tend to destabilize
her behavior, allowing hostile-aggressive actions to emerge.

THE DEVELOPMENT OF ATTRIBUTIONAL STYLE

How children's development may shape their control beliefs is still a matter of great contention. Nicholls (1978) and
Germain (1985) have suggested that developmental considerations may factor heavily in children's control orientation.
If this is the case, we would expect to see some normal
evolution in children's control orientation. Whether such a
pattern exists at all and what it looks like are still open to
dispute. Several researchers (e.g., Lawrence & Winschel,
1975; Mischel, Zeiss, & Zeiss, 1974) have concluded that
locus of control does evolve in a discernible way during early
childhood. Weisz & Stipek (1982) reviewed the available literature on locus of control in children and found that theorists
were divided as to whether the perceived control becomes
more internal or more external with age. Some studies supported the view that the child's developing competence is
reflected in a more internal locus of control (Lefcourt, 1976;
Linn & Hodge, 1982). Other studies (Rotter, 1966) supported
the position that young children have illusory ideas of contingency relationships between their actions and the real
world; thus, with advancing age, they show an increasing
awareness of the world as being contingent on external factors. Still other researchers (Hegland & Galejs, 1983; Galejs
& Hegland, 1982) contend that there is no proof of a develop-

mental trend and that locus of control orientation is a stable trait by preschool age.

Among those who see a developmental progression from externality to internality, there has been a strong attempt to link this trend with cognitive development. Despite the intuitive appeal of such a relationship, many studies have challenged it. Hegland and Galejs (1983), for example, studied 177 preschoolers (mean age 55 months) longitudinally to determine how cognitive factors, as well as social agents, affect locus of control in children. Their observation that most children become decentered by the age of four or five, but that many still do not develop internal locus of control, led them to conclude that egocentrism and locus of control are independent variables.

Older populations do not display any greater correlation between cognitive development and locus of control, as the work of Germain (1985) reveals. He conducted a study to determine the presence of an "integrated" locus of control in a group of junior high school students and a group of college students. Each subject was tested using Rotter's "I-E Scale" (1966) for measuring internal versus external locus of control, an intelligence test (Weschler, 1955), and an instrument devised by Germain to measure "integrated locus of control." As expected, Germain found the incidence of abstract reasoning, as evidenced on both the intelligence test and the "integrated locus of control" measure, to be higher in college students. However, he found relatively little correlation between age and locus of control as measured by Rotter's instrument. Similarly, Wallace and Fonte (1984) found little correlation between locus of control and the level of abstract reasoning in samples of seven, ten, and thirteen-year-olds.

These studies notwithstanding, there is still some strong evidence that cognitive development has a strong effect on the development of locus of control orientation. Indeed, Jones (1978) has demonstrated that one measure of cognitive development, conservation, could predict locus of control orientation. In a longitudinal study of 38 children tested first when they were in kindergarten and first grade, and subsequently when they were fourth and fifth graders, he found that early concepts of conservation did predict locus of control.

Greater interest, however, has centered on how the transition from an egocentric to a decentered perspective may affect control beliefs. The cognitive ability to perceive the interaction of various internal and external factors develops with age. In this model, the child in the concrete operations stage of cognitive development (Piaget, 1929) is able to attribute events to single causes, either internal or external. As the child reaches the formal operations stage, he or she is able to understand interactive models of causation, including both internal and external factors. Germain refers to this as an "integrated" locus of control.

Before children have developed an integrated locus of control, however, certain logical misperceptions may actually help to protect them from experiencing a lack of control. Young children's failure to distinguish between interrelated causes and their tendency to generalize causes (Kun, 1977; Nicholls, 1978) may serve to protect their sense of competence and self-esteem. Often young children attribute a positive outcome to both high effort and high ability and a negative outcome to both low effort and low ability. This phenomenon, which the researchers call a "halo schema," leads the child to feel a sense of competence only if a task requires considerable exertion; without such effort, the success will not engender a feeling of competence (Kun, 1977). Older children (approximately nine years and up) are able to use a "compensatory schema" which allows them to attribute an outcome to either high effort and low ability or vice versa. Thus, the tendency to avoid stable and global attributions implied by the "halo schema" may insulate a child from the effects of learned helplessness.

It seems possible that Lisa's risk of depression about her mother's leave of absence may be somewhat exacerbated due to the halo schema process. Since she is accustomed to expending great effort in learning her school lessons and her music, she may be hampered in her ability to derive satisfaction from achievements less dearly won. This would decrease the number of opportunities for self-esteem through feelings of mastery and may lower her overall resiliency about her mother's leavetaking.

On the other hand, according to Piaget and others (Piaget, 1929; Piaget & Inhelder, 1975), young children have difficulty perceiving events as totally noncontingent, and thus may attribute chance events such as the death of a loved one to some contingent cause, perhaps in themselves. Nevertheless, this tendency appears to decline with age. Weisz & Stipek's review (1982) found that the degree of illusory contingency declined with development and maturation. Young children may not perceive chance in the same way as adults do, so that chance outcomes are perceived as controllable; "luck" may be perceived as an internal, rather than an external, factor.

This view of declining illusory contingency is by no means beyond dispute. There is some evidence that many of the cognitive distortions such as illusory contingency thought to be unique to children — and thought to offer them some protection against the deficits produced by learned helplessness — may persist well into adulthood. Research by Langer (1975) and others demonstrated that many adults commonly perceive chance events (such as the roll of a pair of dice) as being contingent upon internal qualities. While this phenomenon is usually interpreted as the overinternalizing of locus of control in response to positive outcomes, Rothbaum, Weisz, and Snyder see it as a form of illusory control in those with an external locus of control. Illusory contingency serves an adaptive function, allowing people to share in perceived control of others. Attribution of events to "luck" (Lefcourt, 1976; Phares, 1976) is another means of identifying with a controlling factor.

Attributions to powerful others are similar to attributions to luck, in that they both permit the individual to share in a perceived control. "Vicarious control" includes identification with a larger group, such as one's nation or religious affiliation. This type of perceived control is also the basis for identification with a powerful aggressor or demagogue. Such a phenomenon is an example of submissive behavior in the service of perceived control.

All of the above attributions (predictive control, illusory control, vicarious control) are termed by Rothbaum and associates to be types of "interpretive control" (Frankl, 1963; Garber, Miller, & Abramson, 1980; Rothbaum, et al., 1982). Any attempt to interpret events so as to better understand and accept them is seen as a means of gaining control over those events, even when no primary control is possible.

Whether or not illusory contingency declines with age, rendering children more susceptible to feelings of helplessness, children do appear to have other logical misperceptions that discourage the internal, stable, and global attributional style described by Abramson, et al., (1978). In reviewing the perception of competence, Weisz and Stipek cite Ruble, Parsons, & Ross (1976), who showed that preschool and early elementary grade children are less likely than children in the later elementary grades and up to assess their competence relative to that of classmates. The tendency not to make comparative judgments of ability relates to the attribution of universal or specific control, that is, whether a peer would find the same situation controllable or not.

The seeming instability of children's ability attributions may also buffer them temporarily from the potential ramifications of such an explanatory style. Children's conception of ability appears to undergo a change at about the age of seven years. Prior to this age, children tend to see ability, and intelligence in particular, as an additive function which can be increased by increasing effort or learning a specific skill. After this age, ability is viewed as a more stable, global characteristic which can be compared to that of peers. A perception of ability as a transient quality makes failure appear less stable. Young children (under seven years) also tend to view their performance much less realistically than older children. Several researchers (Marshall, Weinstein, Middlestadt, & Brattesani, 1980; Stipek, 1981a) have found that most kindergarten and first-grade children rank themselves at or near the top of their class, although their ratings of other children tend to be in accord with the teacher's ratings. Children over seven years tend to rate themselves along the same lines as their teachers. Also, young children tend to maintain higher performance expectations in the face of repeated failures (Parsons & Ruble, 1977). They are thus less susceptible to the effects of learned helplessness (Weisz, 1981). Indeed, Rholes, Blackwell, Jordan, and Walters (1980) suggest that children whose mental age is under nine and a half are less likely to view ability as a stable factor. Young children in learning activities have a greater tolerance for repeated failure without loss of self-esteem, according to Parsons and Ruble (1977), who found that older children base their expectations of success or failure on past experience more than young children do. Three-year-olds in this study did not significantly change their expectations of success or failure even after repeated failures. Ruble et al. (1976) also found that kindergartners' perceptions of their levels of ability were less affected by success or failure than those of seven – to nine-year-olds.

With regard to perception of ability level, Lisa is probably well in advance of the norm – at least in terms of mastering external tasks such as reading and playing music. She has plenty of evidence that she is doing things few children her age can do. While Lisa's competences give her some reason to feel masterful and secure in her abilities, her mastery of internal tasks such as impulse control is on a much lower level. Thus, the two domains exist in uneasy disequilibrium, possibly confusing her attempts to develop an attributional style.

ENVIRONMENTAL INFLUENCES ON ATTRIBUTIONAL STYLE

While the role of the normal course of development in shaping perceptions of control is still far from clear, this is less the case with respect to environmental factors. Investigations of the environmental factors responsible for one's control beliefs have been more convincing, although far from conclusive. Smith and Bain (1978), who studied kindergarten children and discerned no significant relationship between locus of control and such factors as ethnic group, income level, or educational level, are among the few to minimize the significance of environmental factors. Studies by Franklin (1963) and Battle and Rotter (1963) found differences in locus of control associated with socioeconomic status. Both children and adults of higher socioeconomic level measured as being more internally oriented.

Perhaps the greatest area of certainty surrounds the importance of caregivers in determining a young child's perceptions of control. Theoretical literature has, as we have seen, documented the importance of caregivers to the infant's experience of contingency. A variety of research has shown that parental attitudes and behaviors continue to serve as the medium in which children form their beliefs about control. Children in different child-care settings tend to display differences in locus of control orientation (Norris, 1980). Seligman and Peterson (1986; Seligman et al., 1984) found that the attributional style of depressed mothers (depression assessed by the Beck Depression Inventory [Beck, Ward, & Mendelson, 1961]) was correlated more strongly with their children's attributional styles than children's depression was correlated with depression in either parent. Among fifth to eighth graders, Abraham and Christopherson (1984) found a strong correlation between supportive parental behaviors (nurturance, principled discipline, encouragement of autonomy) and the children's perceived competence. Punitive behaviors, by contrast, led to lesser degrees of perceived competence.

Not surprisingly, divorce has been linked with externality of LOC in some research. Wiehe (1984) found that children aged nine to fifteen from homes in which divorce had occurred were significantly more external in their locus of control beliefs than children from intact homes. Differences between the two groups were particularly prominent among the youngest children studied. Children who have experienced a marital disruption as being beyond their control may generalize this perception to other life experiences, thereby impeding the development of what Wiehe sees as the natural progression to greater internality over the course of early development.

Wiehe's (1986) recent study of children removed from the custody of their parents further confirms these conclusions. When he compared the locus of control orientations of a group of pregnant adolescents in foster care to a group of pregnant adolescents from intact families, he found the former significantly more external in their orientation. Based on the study, however, it is unclear which specific aspects of the apparent family interactional difficulties – breakup of the family or the actual placement in foster care – were responsible for the greater externality of this group.

Whether children of divorced parents and disruptive home environments are more or less internally oriented than children of intact marriages is still not beyond dispute, however. For example, Kalter, Alpern, Spence, and Plunkett (1984) found greater internality among third-fifth grade children of divorced parents than among their counterparts from intact homes. The investigators suggest that this observed internality may reflect a defense against feelings of helplessness associated with the divorce or the application of these children's as yet egocentric thinking to an understanding of the reasons for their parents' divorce.

Harsh home environments in which parents are unresponsive to children may also lead to atypical control orientation. Children in homes where abuse has occurred are significantly more external than nonabused children (Ellis and Milner, 1981; Slade et al., 1984). Apparently such differences are more pronounced with respect to attributions for failure than for success. While abused and nonabused children in Slade et al.'s study took equal responsibility for successes, the former took significantly less control for failures than did the latter. The authors suggest that denying responsibility for failure and projecting blame onto the environment may serve as a defense against the threatening prospect of punishment. Although abused children may compare favorably to nonabused children in their persistence, they may apply themselves more concertedly when pursuing a desired outcome than when avoiding an undesired one.

Since Lisa's parents might be overachievers to some degree, it is possible they are combatting, through mastery of difficult tasks, negative feelings resulting from an external locus of control. If true, Lisa may be at risk on several levels. First, the high correlation between maternal and child attributional styles carries the risk that Lisa might develop a predominantly external LOC regardless of her level of mastery. This risk is further exacerbated by the fact that her parents' divorce was an event that occurred entirely outside of her control. Now, once again, her parents are about to be apart. Certainly Lisa is entitled to some sadness and anxiety.

CONCLUSION AND FINAL ASSESSMENT

Lisa's main area of risk is the early and profound experience of lack of contingency/control triggered by her separation experiences. It is apparent that her locus of control is predominantly internal in terms of her interaction with the nonsocial environment (academic problem-solving, etc.). With regard to her less internal LOC in peer situations, it must be remembered that she is the only child of divorced parents, both of whose temperaments are somewhat withdrawn.

Furthermore, Lisa's parents have placed high demands on her in terms of nonsocial achievements. Accordingly, Lisa has devoted a great deal of attention to meeting her parents' intrinsically nonsocial goals. This, in combination with the fact that she is an only child and is experiencing anxiety over yet another separation experience, goes a long way toward explaining her current social difficulties. Lisa's attributional style is a healthy one, revealing that she attributes the outcome of events largely to her own actions and does not become drastically upset when an outcome is negative. However, there may be significant exceptions to this general internal scheme. Lisa may well be blaming herself for her mother's departure once again. Repeated separations have put Lisa at risk for developing a sense of contingency that is discontinuous when dealing with her mother, the primary figure in her life. Lisa may feel that the rule of contingency with its associated features of predictability, safety, and control pertains to every aspect of her life except for the one factor that matters most: her mother's behavior.

Lisa would have good reason for feeling this way, since the reality of the situation is that nothing she does will prevent her mother from leaving. In this solitary but powerful sector of her life, Lisa may be experiencing feelings analogous to those encountered in learned helplessness situations, since none of her actions directed at escape from more separation trauma has proved effective.

This situation represents a fairly significant threat to Lisa's well-being. While Lisa is a bright child, strongly motivated in both internal and external domains, it will be important to protect her from any further significant stress following her mother's leave of absence. In order to help Lisa fend off the urge to withdraw into apathy and sadness resulting from her inability to influence her mother's decision, her father must be especially supportive. In addition, it will be helpful if her mother makes regular contact with Lisa by phone calls and audiotapes. With sufficient love and support from this quarter, Lisa should be able to develop in the face of this strongly negative episode of noncontingency. This growth process will be provided with extra fuel as Lisa goes on with school and is provided with increased opportunities for social interaction and mastery.

5

PLAY BEHAVIOR

This case addresses the question of when the normally energetic play of the young child crosses the line into aggression, becoming a sign of psychopathology.

JEFF

Jeff is a three-year-old child, the youngest of three sons. His father is a physician and his mother works as an interior decorator from the home. The child was initially brought in for evaluation by both parents because, as Jeff's father explained, his son tended to alternate between solitary and aggressive behaviors at the preschool he had been attending for two months. Jeff's mother tended to minimize the importance of the problem, noting, "He's always been the quiet one in the family. I think sometimes my husband pushes him too much."

Throughout the interview the child appeared excessively withdrawn. Although he gravitated toward the toy cabinet, he played with the toys in an indiscriminate and desultory fashion. Significantly, his mother intermittently gazed in his direction. Several times when Jeff picked up a toy, she would say softly, "No honey, play with the truck instead." At one point, she stopped speaking mid-sentence, rose abruptly and went over to her son, who had picked up some crayons. Grabbing the crayons from his hands, she said, "You shouldn't play with these; you will mess up your new pants."

After that incident Jeff's mother resumed her seat and conversation continued for several minutes. Suddenly, the child leapt up and began running around the room clutching a miniature race car, while yelling "zoom, zoom." Almost immediately, Jeff's mother placed her hands over her ears. "Jeff, don't do that," she said, "you are making a racket again and we can't hear ourselves think." The child did not respond, ceasing the activity only when the therapist spoke to him in a gentle voice. Upon being asked later why he had chosen to play with the race car, Jeff indicated that he wanted to be a driver and go very fast so he wouldn't be caught. When Jeff's mother was asked to comment on this, she observed, "I don't know why he's so disruptive."

NORMAL EXUBERANCE OR CONDUCT DISORDER

Is Jeff a normally exuberant three-year-old or is his aggressive play behavior indicative of a more deep-seated psychopathologic problem, such as a Conduct Disorder of the Solitary Aggressive Type as described in *DSM-III-R*? The criteria for such a Conduct Disorder include deliberate destruction of the property of others and a persistent pattern of behavior in which rules for that age group are violated. From the above description it does not appear that Jeff's behavior is that extreme. Nevertheless, his outburst of aggression in front of the therapist and his parents—as evidenced by his overzealous noisemaking and refusal to obey his mother—suggests that Jeff may be experiencing some problems which he is not yet capable of expressing verbally.

As will be seen, one way of exploring the etiology of a child's disruptive behavior is to focus on play activities. Through the enactment of play scenarios, the child may be better able to express, in symbolic fashion, some of his inner turmoil and conflict. In this case, conflict arose largely from the incapacity of Jeff's mother to fully comprehend the child's natural tendency to engage in play. During the intake interview, she persisted in interrupting Jeff each time he selected a toy. The crayons were no good because he might get messy; similarly, the toy racing car was inappropriate because Jeff made too much noise when playing with it. What this caregiver failed to understand was that preschoolers must be permitted to engage in play behaviors of their choice in order to develop adaptively. Indeed, it is through play that the child learns the very process of choice and of selecting various courses of action. By stifling her son's native capacity to experiment with the world around him by engaging in play, Jeff's mother was, in essence, creating impediments to his developmental capacities. As is discussed below, play is instrumental in helping the child assimilate such concepts as intentionality, object differentiation, and ultimately, symbolic thought. Thus, treatment here should concentrate on helping the caregiver understand that allowing her son to play in an encouraging atmosphere will promote his development and is in fact essential to that development.

NORMAL PLAY BEHAVIOR

Q: What's the one thing you like to do best?
A: Play!

Play is of immense developmental importance for the simple reason that it provides the young child with his or her richest source of learning. Play situations are the primary means through which a child is first able to make and coordinate the all-important distinctions between appearance and reality. The importance, as well as the complexity, of play is demonstrated by the fact that the Oxford unabridged dictionary devotes nearly five pages to its definition. For our purposes here, play as children practice it has three main characteristics: (1) an expression of wishes and fantasies; (2) enactment of these wishes in an attempt at fulfillment; and (3) awareness of its nonreality (Neubauer, 1987). These three fundamental properties of play are contained in four generally agreed upon types of play behavior: (1) sensorimotor play (however, this earliest non-associative manipulation of objects can only barely qualify as play per se); (2) mastery play;

(3) make-believe or symbolic play; and (4) games with rules (Singer, 1979). The various types of play and their universal components will provide Jeff with the opportunity to practice assimilation and accommodation (Piaget, 1962) as he proceeds toward establishing a workable reality construct through understanding the difference between appearance and reality in social and physical environments.

As Neubauer (1987) points out, the fact that play demands enactment is what provides the clinician with a therapeutic and communicative tool for engaging in interaction with the child. In Jeff's case, this communicative/therapeutic link needs to be bolstered by imbuing the act of play itself with a more pleasurable valence. Once this was achieved by (1) reducing his mother's somewhat demanding presence, (2) providing a more pleasurable assortment of toys, and (3) supplying encouragement by being admiring and allowing him to be passive in order to acknowledge his dependency needs, Jeff's attitude toward play, as well as his affect in general, improved markedly.

In Jeff's case, as in all children, it is play that buffers the transition from conformity with the pleasure principle to living according to the reality principle. In order to achieve this transition, play is both active (exploration) and reactive (escape from the demands of reality). These properties enable eventual mastery of the external environment. In addition, play is a normal activity—but one that may have pathologic features. When the same play occurs over a long period because the child cannot find a solution to the "play" problem posed, this may signal a pathologic conflict or developmental deviation.

FUNCTIONAL ASPECTS OF PLAY

Q: What kind of play do you like best?
A: (As Jeff answers the therapist, he becomes more and more animated) Pretend.
Q: Pretend with cars?
A: Yes.

Q: Pretend with dolls?
A: No!
Q: Pretend with blocks?
A: Yeah!
Q: You like to play with blocks. Big ones or little ones?
A: Big ones! So I can climb!

During the initial interview, and in several play sessions after, Jeff displayed no tendency to fixate on one mode of play, nor did he persevere on any one play problem. Thus, by this broad measure, Jeff appears to be age-normal, with no overt pathology. An examination of play from the viewpoint of a normally developing child like Jeff will help in comprehending the major facultative contributions made by pretend activities.

Singer (1973) has noted that play provides the developing child with an immediate coping mechanism through which the child can act out and rehearse behaviors that have yet to be mastered in real life. Additionally, play provides a vehicle through which children can distance themselves from their environment and gain the benefit of a different perspective (Fein, 1981). Fink (1976) has emphasized the fact that each context presents a new challenge; thus, every play situation that the child represents internally must be reconciled with the physical environment in which the child wishes to express these roles and to make them both credible and acceptable. In this way, the child's play and the resultant appearance-reality distinctions created in the play scenario are the outcome of a synthesizing process in which internal states are reconciled with external "reality."

Within the psychoanalytic perspective, play is viewed as contributing to learning by means of disinhibition. For example, Levin and Turgeon (1957) argue that play is the means through which children can release emotions that they cannot express in real life. This is in accord with Freud's original formulations, in which the symbolic nature of play is regarded as being the result of unmet, infantile desires (Freud, 1909, 1922). Through play, the child can master the conflict, anxiety, tension, and guilt associated with these desires. In other words, by experiencing a play environment which is both nonthreatening and controllable, the child has the opportunity to experiment with acting-out against what he or she has passively accepted in real life (Freud, 1932).

Cognitive developmentalists view the benefits of play in yet another way. De-emphasizing the emotional components proposed by the psychoanalytic view, cognitive theorists focus more intensely on play as an expression of the child's level of sophistication in handling symbols (Hulme & Lunzer, 1966; Piaget, 1962; Watson & Fischer, 1977). Within the cognitive developmental framework, it is not so much intrusion from the outside world, but the maturity of the child's representational abilities that inhibits play. That is, the more immature the child's symbolic abilities, the more real-life situations promote play in an attempt to gain perspective and mastery; conversely, real-life situations inhibit play in the presence of more mature representational abilities.

At this juncture it should be noted that both the psychoanalytic and cognitive developmental viewpoints on the nature and function of play point to the importance of living in an environment that is conducive to and encourages play. Play (and hence learning) becomes restricted as a function of increasing intrusion from the outside world (e.g., stress or an overly controlling caregiver). In terms of offering ample opportunity to play, Jeff's environment is fine. However, his overall ability to learn through play might be somewhat decreased by the intense and somewhat intrusive concern of his mother.

Role-playing provides a good example of the fundamental task of play in learning. Developing infants make judgments about their own internal states based on their perceptions of caregivers' reactions. As they grow older, children take on more and more roles in order to compare and contrast their sense of themselves against the viewpoints of others (Corsaro, 1979). In this way, the child gradually assumes the responsibilities and perceptions of another person while retaining his or her real-life perspective. Thus, the crucially important task of self-object differentiation is greatly facilitated (Fink, 1981).

In sum, pretend play provides the child with a limitless number of possible situations and resultant transformations that furnish the child with an abundance of new meanings and contexts in which to dwell and learn (Baldwin, 1911). Play is an active behavior that is performed by the child expressly for his/her own purposes, the experience of playing being inherently more important than its end result (Bruner, 1972; Piaget, 1962; Vandenberg, 1978). However, the extent to which a child actively plays – and learns – is dependent upon the level of environmental stress (e.g., economic privation, abuse) and the overall degree of support and interest the primary caregiver displays towards the child's play activities (Gershowitz, 1974; Singer, 1977). While the parent's presence during play may inhibit the child's pretending ability, the parent's approval and empathic response to the child's pretense remain an important aspect of the child's play environment. Overall, Jeff appears to have the advantage of parents who are enthusiastic about his achievements and who are generally supportive. However, it is possible that overattentiveness on the part of his mother and her emphasis on "practical toys" have somewhat inhibited the quality and/or frequency of Jeff's play activities.

The fact that play is important within the context of learning makes it equally important in the clinical setting. While young children lack adults' mature capacity to hide emotions behind a complex network of defenses – a clinical advantage, they also lack the verbal skills to convey their internal state – a clinical disadvantage. The analysis of play behaviors not only circumvents the problem of the child's limited verbal communication skill but also provides valuable insights about the fundamental way in which the child views the world. In short, play provides a rich diagnostic and therapeutic context in which the trained observer can analyze unconscious processes during "pretend" situations, thereby diagnosing and treating areas of confusion or conflict.

DEVELOPMENTAL ASPECTS OF PLAY

Q: Do you ever play with soldier dolls?

A: (smiling) Yeah!

Q: When they fight, do they ever get scared?

A: Sometimes they do.

Q: What happens when they get scared? Do you make them fight anyway?

A: (Jeff becomes serious) They have to fight. They can't get away.

Q: Do they get killed?

A: No! They win!

The developmental functions of play are multifaceted. During play the child learns to master and organize his past experiences and thoughts into a complex symbolic network. Play gives the child opportunities for expressing emotions and exerting control over what might be uncontrollable and/ or fearful circumstances in real life. Scaling thoughts and conflicts down to these symbolic play enactments allows the child to begin to master the situation. Not only does play enhance the organization of thought, but the ways in which the child organizes his/her thoughts are evident to the clinician observing the child. It is unfortunate that no definitive analysis of play exists to provide us with an exact measure of the child's developmental condition. However, by keeping in mind the various symbolic and adaptational aspects of play diagnosed by many observers and several theorists, the clinician can still use it as a valuable barometer for evaluating the child's overall functional capacity.

For example, Fink (1976) defined the useful aspects of play based upon five psychological functions, each of which acts as an organizer for the child's thoughts. The child:

(1) through integration and modification of experience, develops coherent roles and extended plots;

(2) gains the ability to relate a part to a whole and represent a theme through complex symbolic forms;

(3) creates conflicts between disparate and disagreeing roles or beliefs as a means of mastering interpersonal conflicts that play a role in the environment;

(4) experiments with language, communicating in dialogues; and

(5) through spontaneous and uninhibited play, "works out" and "thinks through" problems evolving during critical stages of this thematic development.

The clinician may see in play the young child's repertoire of knowledge and experience.

Singer (1979) concurs that play provides a means of organization, positing that play may allow the child to fuse language and imagery storing processes. Paivio (1970) and Witelson (1976) hypothesized that imagery and language are stored and organized separately within the brain, but according to Rohwer (1967), these processes interact to establish a greater system of organization and storage. Thus, play may provide the opportunity for the systems of language and images to interact. The child, attempting to master an internal symbolic representational system, creates imaginative situations in which he acts out these representations in the form of play (Singer, 1973, 1979).

Singer's findings have consistently demonstrated links between the level of three-to-four-year-olds' pretend play and their language development. The child's ability to develop cohesive "anticipatory guiding images, verbal labels, and plans with easily spun-out subroutines" (Singer, 1979, p. 16) relies heavily on the child's human experiences and his abilities to transfer that knowledge into the pretense behaviors that best represent and communicate his thoughts.

Jeff appears well able to transfer his knowledge into new situations. For example, in role-playing, Jeff demonstrated his ability to discriminate between identities of meaningful others and the roles they enact, just as he is learning to discriminate between his own self and the roles he can enact. Relevant to these observations is the fact that some of the most dramatic results obtained from research involving story-enactment training are accompanied by a diminished sense of egocentricity (Ianotti, 1978; Rosen, 1974; Saltz, Dixon, & Johnson, 1977; Smith & Sydall, 1978). Thus, by being able to assume the roles of others and the limitations of those roles (e.g., the car took on an impersonal, monotonic voice), Jeff demonstrates that he has achieved a good level of separation and individuation from his caregivers and from his early childhood egocentricity.

DIAGNOSTICALLY USEFUL ASPECTS OF PLAY

Q: If we were playing a game, would you rather be Superman or the Hulk?
A: The Hulk!
Q: Why would you rather be the Hulk?
A: 'Cause he doesn't have to talk to anyone.

Play serves as a diagnostic tool useful in assessing the child's level of development. In order to fully employ this observational technique for a given child, the age-specific aspects of play must be understood.

Chronology of Play Behaviors

In dissecting the development of play behavior, Parten (1932) postulated six categories of play based on a scale of social interaction in children between the ages of two and five. The six categories were defined as follows:

(1) unoccupied behavior—the child observes the events occurring around him and displays interest, but makes no effort to become an active participant;

(2) onlooker—the child spends the vast majority of time observing others' play activities, only occasionally verbalizing questions or suggestions;

(3) solitary play—the child plays, but alone, to the exclusion of other children;

(4) parallel activity—the child plays alone, but uses toys and objects similar to those used by the children around him/her;

(5) associative play – the child engages in play with other children, although the play is not necessarily identical in nature, and is not goal- or product-oriented;

(6) cooperative play – the child plays with other children in order to achieve a goal through competition, formal games, the creation of a product, or role-playing.

From her observations, Parten concluded that the amount of social interaction during play increases as the chronological age of the child increases. Younger children were found to engage in more of the unoccupied behavior, onlooker, and solitary play types, while the older children's play behaviors were more likely to be categorized as parallel activity, associative play, and cooperative play. Iwanaga (1973), in refining these findings somewhat, found that the child's ability to engage in cooperative play was not evident in three-year-olds, appearing only at the age of four.

Jeff preferred the solitary Hulk to the more gregarious Superman, but he does not engage in parallel play according to his preschool teacher. As yet, he has not progressed to cooperative play activities. It might prove valuable to watch for this cooperative play behavior sometime during this fourth year of his life in order to assure his continued age-normative development.

Singer's (1979) four play categories, which occur in sequence – (1) sensorimotor; (2) mastery; (3) symbolic; and (4) games with rules – are reminiscent of those in a study by Smilansky (1968). He defined four categories of play thought to develop in a predetermined sequence: (1) functional play – simple actions or gestures either with or without objects; (2) constructive play, organization, and/or use of objects in order to achieve an end product or goal; (3) dramatic play – the appearance of the pretend (as if) situation to fulfill the child's personal wishes and needs; and (4) games with rules – the understanding and acceptance of predetermined, conscious rules in an organized situation.

Examining Parten's categories of play development in conjunction with Smilansky's categories, Rubin, Maioni, and Hornung (1976) created the Parten-Smilansky Play Scale. These investigators studied three- and four-year-old children from middle- and lower-class environments and found that solitary play was cognitively and socially more developed than parallel play in this group. This finding is relevant to assessing Jeff's development because, as the researchers suggest, the child in the parallel play situation may want to play with other children but may not have the ability to do so in a sharing and cooperative fashion. They suggest that the child who plays alone is doing so intentionally, with the desire to distance himself from others in order to engage in play without arousing conflict. Jeff's play behaviors indicate that he may be at a somewhat, but not alarmingly, lower level of cognitive/emotional development than what seemed at first to be the case.

It is interesting to note that children from lower socioeconomic groups engaged in more parallel and functional play and less associative, cooperative, or constructive play than did their middle-class counterparts. The researchers posit that middle-class children may engage in more dramatic and constructive play than their peers from lower socioeconomic groups because the middle-class children have more toys and activities at home, and therefore can practice and master their skills earlier. If this explanation applies, Jeff's predominantly parallel play behavior at age three may be the result of the overstressing of practical toys. Furthermore, as noted earlier, play development can also be inhibited by intrusion from the environment, and the overattentiveness of Jeff's mother may be hindering her son's development somewhat.

Fein's observations also provide some help in determining the degree of Jeff's development vis-a-vis play. Fein (1979) has noted that, up until the age of three years, children's play is solitary in nature — seldom does the child under three years of age interact with another child in play, although a shared sequence may appear occasionally in the form of mirroring behaviors. Fein has documented the fact that at 36 months sociodramatic play develops for the first time. By age five, the child has mastered his sensorimotor play sequences and is developing the ability to integrate knowledge concerning reciprocal roles, complex plots, and a vast array of objects and meanings into coherent themes. While Jeff is not functioning at the five-year-old level, he is demonstrating some ability to perform sociodramatic play, as demonstrated by his behavior at preschool. As with cooperative play behavior, it may be advisable to monitor Jeff during the fourth year to see if age-appropriate integrative abilities with reciprocal roles and complex plots begin to develop.

COMPONENTS OF PLAY

Q: Do you like toys that have moving parts, like the wheels on a car, or do you like ones like building blocks?
A: I like cars!
Q: What else do you like?
A: I like trains and soldiers.
Q: Do you have a lot of these kinds of toys at home?
A: (resignedly) No. Mommy likes me to play with Legos.

Further delineations of chronological age and play behaviors, however limited, do exist and must be examined in relation to their specific variables and functions. Discussion here will center on an examination of play behavior in relation to four of its most significant components: object differentiation, role-playing, representation of symbols and self, and intentionality. Examination of these four components will serve reasonably well in completing the picture of play as it relates to the diagnosis of an infant or young child's development.

Object Differentiation

The first aspect to be addressed in this section is object differentiation. The child who cannot separate meaning from object or meaning from action clearly may be at risk for cognitive and emotional problems. The object in play is generally agreed to serve as a medium upon which the child can displace his thoughts and/or act out his feelings. Thus, in order for the child to play effectively (i.e., to learn), the child must have access to objects that maintain his interest (Rubin, Fein, & Vandenberg, 1983). Here again, we see Jeff has been operating at a deficit. Jeff is experiencing a shortage of *interesting* toys because his mother insists on choosing the toys that suit her purposes more than his.

The object is significant in part because during the sensorimotor stage the child lacks the ability to verbalize his thoughts; therefore, the object becomes the target of all the child's thoughts and actions. Outside of the child's own body, the object is the first vehicle through which the child can express his sense of self in play.

The degree to which the presence of objects affects the child's play behaviors has been examined by Singer (1961) with children of two different age groups. Singer placed each child in a dull situation, asking the child to wait, and leaving him/her with nothing to do. Singer observed that children who may already have developed stable representational abilities were able to create fantasies to alleviate their boredom. In contrast, younger children, who may not have developed a representational model free from the sensorimotor modes of representation, were incapable of escaping from boredom by means of devising fantasies in play. The young child's play behaviors were dependent upon the physical availability of objects in his immediate vicinity (Singer, 1961). Fein (1979) agrees, asserting that as long as the child operates within the sensorimotor stage, he can only function in accord with his immediate environment. Once the ability to internally represent objects develops, the child can then substitute what is in his mind for what he encounters in the immediate surroundings. Further research has indicated that the object presented to the young child in play should bear a resemblance to signified objects encountered in the child's daily life. Substituted objects with little resemblance to their originals may place overwhelming cognitive demands on the child (Elder & Pederson, 1978; Fein, 1979). However, both Piaget (1962) and Vygotsky (1967) have associated the emergence of symbolic play with the acquisition of representational skills. Piaget (1962) even contends that substitution processes (i.e., making a stick into a truck) make important contributions to the development of the child's ability to engage in symbol formation. Therefore, the continuous availability of play objects which accurately duplicate the real-life object may actually retard the child's ability to attribute meaning to objects. This phenomenon may be another possible reason for Jeff's slightly lower-than-expected capacity to play. The surfeit of toys he has to play with at home may not sufficiently challenge his imagination.

Golomb and Cornelius (1977) hypothesize that during play the child retains the object's inherent function and identity — a condition they call "pseudoreversibility," which allows the child to view the object both as itself and as the "signifier" into which it has been transformed. Fein (1979) suggests that the reversibility of objects that emerges during play may correlate with the reversibility found within conservation tasks, tasks that force the child to convert an object from its representative functions back to its original state. In this regard, the development of the child's play progresses from the status of being wholly realistic in the treatment of objects to being characterized by the skill of accepting more abstract attributions and integrating them into a growing representational scheme that eventually comes to resemble a symbol. As seen with Jeff, the child moves from the sensorimotor stage, having developed these abilities, and proceeds into the pretend play activity of role-playing, which further draws upon the pseudo-reversibility of objects.

Role-Playing Behaviors

Although the cognitive implications of role-playing behaviors are probably not clear before age seven (Bigner, 1974; Chambers & Tavuchis, 1976; Elkind, 1962; Emmerich,

1959, 1961; Greenfield & Childs, 1977; Sigel et al., 1967), such behaviors begin to emerge during the second year of life (Watson & Fischer, 1980). This phenomenon coincides directly with the emergence of the child's sense of self. By age two and a half, the child assigns specific social names (i.e., mother, father, doctor) to the roles that he enacts during play (Musatti, 1983). Bateson (1956) posits that the child may not be mastering a particular role but instead achieving an understanding of what a "role" is. The child's concrete understanding of roles (a person can only be a mother, father, doctor) gradually becomes less fixed and attains abstract and flexible qualities as the child begins to depict many more roles during play role-playing; in other words, it tends to proliferate. The ages of two to eight years are spent practicing and examining the nuances of role-playing. The understanding of roles is fundamental to a child's ability to feel socially competent (Watson & Fischer, 1980).

Watson and Fischer (1980) have reported that by 18 months of age most children understand that they can be the agents of an action. The two-year-old can make the doll act independently, as if the doll had a will of its own. Capacity for behavioral roles is evident in three-year-olds, who can make the doll behave according to the activities of a specific role. Beyond this, four-year-olds have the ability to establish and represent social roles in the same situation.

By six years of age, the child can attribute two social roles to a single object—the doll can be both a doctor and a father simultaneously towards a patient who is also his daughter. What begins at one and a half years as the simple act of manipulating the doll becomes more complex and elaborate as the child is better able to view others as distinct individuals acting on their own wills and adhering closely to a wide variety of roles that they play in life. So, as Jeff learns that others can be both a doctor and a father, he learns that he can be both a son and a preschooler, and can become more conscious of his own behaviors as he changes his personal roles (Watson & Fischer, 1980).

*Symbols and Representation
of the Self*

The significance of both object-related and role behaviors for the child's developing sense of self and the world must be examined in relation to symbolic play and its implications for self-representation. Relational, or sensorimotor play occurring during the ages of 12-24 months (Fein, 1979; Fenson, Kagan, Kearsley, & Zelazo, 1976) is the precursor of symbolic play. It involves interactions between two objects during a child's play, either in the form of accommodative relational acts (e.g., touching a spoon to a pot lid), or similar groupings (e.g., placing two pot lids together). Relational play appears during the final quarter of the first year, coinciding with stage four object permanence (Piaget, 1952), increased attention to discrepant events (Kagan 1972), and fear of strangers (Fenson et al., 1976; Morgan & Ricciuti, 1967). Kagan (1972) contends that relational play emerges as a result of the child's recently developed ability to combine and/or compare discrepant/similar activities and objects. Relational play therefore may be a behavioral manifestation of this complex organizational process, reflecting the child's recognition of discrepant events in the environment.

Vygotsky (1962) posits that symbolic play behavior is the catalyst which promotes the shift from viewing playthings as objects of action to viewing playthings as objects of symbolic thought. Thus, during relational play, the child views things as objects of action – objects that can be banged together and placed within or on top of one another. The child is unable to separate meaning from object as in symbolic play, and views the object as part of the action itself – the object acquires its meaning solely from the activity it is used to perform. Symbolic play takes objects a step further, placing them in the realm of language and lending to them a significance both personal and possibly incomprehensible to the child's own self. The two-to-three-year-old child now has the ability to separate the object from the action, and can transform objects into symbol representations of his thoughts. For example, a stick may be transformed into a gun in the child's imagination; the toy object is then endowed with the qualities the child has come to associate with guns.

For the child, symbols define the world, while meanings are gained through relationships, associations, and/or conventions with the signified object. As Fein has stated, "Play symbols have a special status because they are derived from imitation, and indicate that the child is coming to grips with the configural properties of situation" (1979, p. 211). Although language, the means through which the child expresses his thoughts, may be arbitrary, the symbols the child uses through language are far from arbitrary, and are generally derived from the child's own personal experiences. Thus, Jeff's desire for the fast-paced life of a race car driver may reveal underlying boredom or a symbolic desire for escape. Thus, for the child, symbolic play may serve as a form of language: It is through coding, organizing, planning, and controlling his actions that the child can create a symbolic, highly intellectual language (Fein, 1979; Piaget, 1962; Vygotsky, 1962) which can act as the vehicle for representing discrete objects and events far removed from the literal meaning generally attributed to the objects.

A strict interpretation of the child's symbolic play may not be possible, however. As assimilation and accumulation of symbols take place, symbols can be subjected to distortions evolving both from past symbols and from the immediate circumstances surrounding the child (Fein, 1979; Gould, 1972; Peller, 1954; Waelder, 1933). Indeed, distortions are bound to occur. Fein (1979) notes that pretense is marked by a "decontexualization" between the child's real-life situations and the play experience. The child is no longer motivated by physical needs (hunger, fatigue) or by the restrictions of routine schedules (naptime, lunch). During play the child controls the factors ordinarily imposed upon him in real life and is thus freed of the specific demands of living. The child's playing motivations and symbols are derived not from real-life contingencies but from emotionally rooted wishes (Overton & Jackson, 1973). In this respect, it is possible that Jeff's fantasies represent a wish to more actively explore his environment in the face of an overprotective mother. Clinicians should be alert to this phenomenon of distortion during play. Unless a complete case history is obtained and the child is questioned about the nature of his play behavior and its significance to him, the symbolic meaning he or she is attributing to play objects and behaviors may be difficult to discern.

Intentionality of Play

The development of intentionality, the ability to discriminate between the intended and unintended results of an action, is crucial if the child is to learn to play and live adaptively. For example, the child who never develops the understanding that self-destructive acts may have an irreversible outcome may be at great risk for suicidal behaviors, or a child who fails to understand the consequences of aggressive behavior may be at risk for antisocial activity.

Kant (1781) argued that humans are born with an idea of causation. This possibly innate notion, which stipulates that an action generates a resulting effect, is termed the generative approach to causation. The young child may not symbolically conceive of the outcome of his actions prior to acting, yet he can still depict the situation internally through representations that allow him to predict or anticipate the outcome of behavior. The child who cannot separate object from action makes the movement of putting his thumb into his mouth. He does not necessarily know that the outcome of the action will be satisfying, but he knows that the action itself is a necessary precursor to the satisfying feeling achieved. The child puts his thumb into his mouth, thereby generating the desired satisfying feeling: thus, "generative transmission forms the basis for casual attribution" (Shultz, 1982b, p. 4). The child's intentionality evolves from the generative state of intending the act to the more causal state of intending the resulting effect of the act (Shultz & Shamash, 1981).

Finding that the two-to-three-year-old has a great deal more knowledge of causation than has been previously recognized, Shultz posits that children can reason about causal phenomena before they can abstract this logical structure for application to purely logical (i.e., noncausal) problems (Shultz, 1982a, 1982b). The causal structure, Shultz contends, is founded upon the bodily experiences of action and perception. The cause of the action is located in the child's environment, and the effect is perceived within the child's mind. This understanding of cause-effect relationships has also been referred to as contingency awareness. Shultz (1980) reported that five-year-olds could distinguish intended and unintended acts and consequences from one another. Shultz and Shamash (1981) further substantiate these findings, noting that by the age of five children can differentiate between intending an action and intending the consequences of that action. However, the extent to which children are conscious of causality has not yet been determined; moreover, we do not know if it remains a hidden perception to be revealed over the course of development. It is also not clear at this point whether or not Jeff can fully understand consequences of his actions. Longitudinal observation of Jeff's behavior during the fourth and fifth years of his life would help resolve this question and provide a clue as to the adequacy of his continuing development.

DUAL CODING: PATHWAY TO
APPEARANCE-REALITY DISTINCTIONS

Q: When you're playing, can a toy do more than one thing? Could a car fly, for instance?

A: Maybe it could, if it was special.

Watson (1986) has proposed a means by which the previously described processes of object differentiation, role-playing, representation of symbols and self, and perception of intentionality coalesce into a single mechanism. This provides the child with the ability to build a functional reality construct (i.e., skill in making appearance-reality distinctions). This mechanism is described as *dual-coding ability*, meaning that children can simultaneously "hold two seemingly incompatible properties or identities in their minds and can apply both properties to the same object or can recognize that one property is perceived or represented by the self and another property is perceived or represented by another person." In other words, "as in other examples of the ability to decentrate [to achieve separation-individuation from the caregiver], children learn to focus on two or more properties of an object and coordinate these various properties" (Flavell et al., 1986, p. 72).

In describing research performed by Flavell et al. (1986), Watson points out that many three-year-olds lack dual-coding ability, as evidenced by their inability to describe what a sponge that looked like a rock looked like. That is, instead of responding that the sponge resembled a rock, they said it was a "sponge," focusing not on the appropriate answer to the question but on what they knew the object to be.

In the same research by Flavell et al., it was found that most three- and four-year-olds were unable to comprehend how two roles (e.g., father, doctor) could be maintained simultaneously by the same person. It appears that, while young children can focus on one property (either of an object or person) at a time, they cannot simultaneously code both appearance and identity (in the case of an object) or two separate roles (in the case of a person) until about age six. Thus, Jeff's richly symbolic but as yet unsophisticated play appears to be age-normal.

CONCLUSION AND FINAL ASSESSMENT

To discuss play is to talk about the child's developmental imperative toward building a viable reality construct — one that allows the individual to correctly perceive the "dos and don'ts" of his physical and social surrounding. At the same time, this construct must not be so rigid that it precludes the creative pursuit of individual hopes and wishes. The "game," whatever it might be, can work either as a challenge to understand reality or as an impediment to learning painful truths.

One good way to assess Jeff's probability of continued learning and mastery is to evaluate the dynamics underlying his need for play and the degree to which play is available to him. As discussed, play provides an immediate coping mechanism, primarily through distancing, when the child is confronted by unmet infantile desires and their associated conflicts, anxieties, and feelings of guilt. This workable, symbolic coping mechanism eventually gives rise to the ability to make accurate distinctions between appearance and reality, because internal representations of objects, relationships, and desires have been brought into alignment with the external physical and emotional worlds by trial and error.

Play is stimulated by the immature conjuring and handling of symbols and inhibited by more highly developed manipulations of symbols. It is also stimulated by lack of intrusion from the environment and by the availability of desirable toys. From these parameters it can be seen that Jeff has only mild interference from his mother to inhibit his play activities and thereby slow his learning process. Thus, in the absence of any repetitive play schemas which might suggest that he is "stuck" on some problem that could prove troublesome later, there seems little reason to conclude that Jeff has a serious problem or that he may be at risk for developing later psychopathology. He has achieved the primary end result of play, that of self-object differentiation, and is well on the way to establishing a good sense of empathy and comprehension of intentionality.

By every major indicator there seems little reason to conclude that Jeff has a serious problem or that he may be at risk of later psychopathology. He has achieved the ability to represent objects and things through play, to draw distinctions or discrepancies, to understand contingency relationships, and to begin manifesting a comprehension of symbolism. The fact that he may be slightly behind his age-level norm in play activities can easily be explained by the inhibitory presence of his mother and perhaps by the fact that he is virtually inundated with toys at home, a condition that might result in below-average self-challenging in play situations.

Jeff does not appear to be overly upset by his mother's intrusiveness, showing an overall secure and adaptive attachment relationship with her. No doubt the fact that his father remains in the home most of the time helps mitigate the intrusiveness of the mother and also provides him with an available male role model. Jeff is expected to develop normally and to catch up to age-appropriate norms very soon, particularly on entry to preschool or school. In this peer flooded environment, Jeff will soon evolve out of solitary play and into social play groups.

In order to insure that adaptive development proceeds in this child, we need to help Jeff's mother understand the significance of role-play behavior in his life. Her overly intrusive attitude has caused him to use play as a form of escape – speeding away in a racing car – rather than as a form of exploration and experimentation. Both of Jeff's parents should be encouraged to attend treatment sessions with their son, so that they can better understand play as an aspect of the developmental process. Only with this realization will Jeff's mother relinquish her control over her son and allow him to use his full developmental potential through play.

6

PROSOCIAL BEHAVIOR

ARTHUR

Arthur is a three-and-a-half-year-old boy brought in for evaluation by his mother, who was concerned about his behavior during the month he had been in preschool. At the initial assessment, Arthur was relatively well behaved, although he fidgeted a good deal and had a noticeable tendency to avoid direct eye contact. His mother, currently pregnant with her second child had become pregnant with Arthur while still in college and dropped out of full-time attendance when she gave birth, because she wanted "to do the right thing" in raising her child. Shortly after the birth, she married Arthur's natural father; the two are still married. Arthur's father remained in school and completed his engineering degree. He is now employed as a civil engineer. During the interview, Arthur's mother reported:

I had a lot of trouble at first accepting the fact that my husband was going to stay in school and I wasn't, but I don't regret what I did—especially since I took correspondence courses later. I'm only a semester away from graduating. But I'm worried about Arthur. He's so agitated when he gets home. Sometimes he's even crying when he gets off the school bus.

While his mother was speaking, Arthur fidgeted continually and once jumped from his chair and sprinted across the room where he stayed for a few seconds before running back to hug his mother's knees. His mother continued:

> His teacher says he'll probably get used to school eventually, but right now he doesn't seem to be playing with the other kids very much. I don't know if it's because he's keeping his distance or if the other kids don't like him. But I do know that he's not getting along as well as he used to with his two friends from the neighborhood. They fight more often than they should. Do you think something could be wrong?

DEVELOPMENT OF PROSOCIAL BEHAVIORS

Several qualities emerge vividly when examining the details of Arthur's intake evaluation. First, the child's demeanor itself is notable: He avoids eye contact with the clinician; even after several minutes of soothing conversation he is unable to gaze directly at the clinician. This hesitation in Arthur's manner is reinforced by his overall withdrawn manner and his mother's comment that he sometimes returns home from school crying. Arthur's recent tendency to become involved in fights with his friends suggests that the child is upset about something. Second, it is notable that Arthur's mother is pregnant and that the change in her son's behavior appears to have coincided with her pregnancy. Indeed, she has only recently begun "showing," and the obvious change in her physical status is likely to have had some connection with the alterations in Arthur's behavior. In addition, Arthur's mother's comments about how she had to leave school prior to her son's birth suggest some regret over the earlier pregnancy.

In an overly zealous attempt to assign psychopathology to the child, one might focus on a diagnosis of either Avoidant Disorder of Childhood or Parent-Child Problem. According to *DSM-III-R*, Avoidant Disorder of Childhood involves excessive shrinking from the contact of unfamiliar people for a period of six months. Parent-Child Problem focuses on a conflict between the parent and child that has come to distort adaptive relations between the two members of the family. Such a problem should be of fairly long-standing duration.

Despite the possibility that Arthur may fulfill the criteria for either or both of these disorders, a closer exploration of this case reveals that this child is attempting to cope with normal feelings that have been aroused by the prospect of a new birth and by his mother's possibly ambivalent feelings towards him. Arthur may feel he is in a particularly precarious emotional position, because just as he is becoming accustomed to exerting autonomy his mother has indicated, through her pregnancy, that he may be replaced. Examination of the development of prosocial behaviors and the need for the child to separate securely from the caregiving figure will be helpful here in reassessing the nature of the attachment relationship.

Q: (tentatively) Ma, I want to see what's in the other room.
A: I don't want you going anywhere without me. Now stay here.

Donne's poetic statement that "no man is an island" is now a matter of accepted scientific fact. In fact, the infant's need to establish attachment bonds with others is equivalent to the need for food in terms of basic drives (Bowlby, 1973, 1980; Minde, 1987). From the first days of birth the infant demonstrates an inherent ability to establish a connection, or bond, between itself and its mother. The infant is able to engage the mother by means of smiling, looking, sucking, and reaching. Because the early attachment to the mother serves as a model or paradigm on which all of his other relationships will come to be based, the sensitivity and consistency of his mother's response to Arthur's overtures as an infant carried ramifications for nearly every aspect of his later interactions with the world (Ainsworth, 1979; Bowlby, 1969, 1973; Cassidy, 1988; Main & Cassidy, 1988; Main, Kaplan, & Cassidy, 1985). The child incorporates experiences with the mother into *working models* and then transfers these models into new relationships. Such a notion explains the continuity of this developmental skill and allows for an explanation of how and why the child organizes his environment.

In a recent study, Plunkett, Klein, and Meisels (1988) demonstrated that securely attached children (as measured in their second year of life) were able at the age of three to interact more positively and socially with an unfamiliar person than were insecurely attached children. Thus, the ability to expand the child's adaptation to the social environment is greatly facilitated by the secure base that the attachment relationship provides.

Efforts to form bonds with others in the world creates a medium that the infant can use in his or her campaign for mastery, the need for which is recognized near the end of the first year of life, when the infant begins to perceive that it is separate from its mother and from every other object in the environment. Through interactions with others (primarily the caregiver at first), the infant can learn the lessons it needs in order to survive. Therefore, the first and foremost goal of a young and struggling human organism is to establish and maintain contact with others, since without others no solutions to survival problems can be found. Hence, the ability to develop prosocial behavior patterns is crucially important; it exists near, or at, the apex of the infant's nascent hierarchy of needs.

Learning to behave in a cooperative fashion with others requires an accurate understanding of self and of the needs of others. These ingredients – self-representation, self-object differentiation, and empathic ability – are greatly dependent on early interactions with the mother within the attachment relationship that evolves between the two. Bowlby (1969), Ainsworth and Wittig (1969), Main et al. (1985) and others, applying an ethological perspective to the relationship between infant and mother, have found that the infant's rapidly burgeoning knowledge first becomes organized in the form of internal working models of self and mother. The greater the accuracy of the working model simulation, the greater will be the likelihood of developing well-adapted behavior.

Under optimal conditions, the attachment relationship allows the infant to use the mother as a secure base for exploration (Ainsworth, 1973; Trad, 1986). The securely attached child can utilize exploration to construct a *self-concept* based on numerous sources of information from the environment. In contrast, an insecurely attached child will feel inhibited in his excursions away from the mother, since the mother fails to make him feel safe unless he is in close proximity to her. Thus, self-object differentiation and the ability to comprehend the needs and intentions of others will suffer if the infant is deprived of opportunities for broad-ranging exploration. There is some concern along these lines for Arthur, since it appears his mother may be inhibiting his urges to explore due to her somewhat overcontrolling urge to "do the right thing."

RAMIFICATIONS OF INSECURE ATTACHMENT ON THE DEVELOPMENT OF PROSOCIAL BEHAVIOR

Q: Do you like building blocks?
A: Yeah!
Q: Did you ever try to build something and it wouldn't stay up?
A: Yeah.
Q: What did you do?
A: (vehemently) I knocked it all down!

The fact that an insecure attachment with the caregiver can easily produce deficits in self-object differentiation (Trad, 1987) leads to the realization that overall cognitive development may be impaired as well, since any system of information is only as good as the mechanism used to construct it. This impaired cognition in insecurely attached infants and children carries serious implications in terms of prosocial behavior development, since inadequate cognitive ability may generate low levels of goal achievement and the resulting frustration experienced by the infant or young child may easily lead to aggressive behavior – a distinctly antisocial activity and one to which Arthur is clearly susceptible.

Aggressive Behavior

Parens (1979) has made useful distinctions among the types of aggressive behavior manifested by young children. There are basically two types of aggression to be alert to; destructive and nondestructive. Destructive aggression is distinctly antisocial in nature because it has a hostile intent directed at entirely eliminating a structure that has proved highly thwarting. The diagnostic question here is whether the child has a legitimate complaint due to the fact that he or she is living in circumstances so disadvantaged that there can be no hope of developing mastery or whether he or she has achieved only a low level of cognitive ability that will disallow mastery under any circumstances. At this point Arthur's aggression with his friends does not seem destructive in intent.

The other category of aggressive behavior posited by Parens – nondestructive – is not hostile in nature. Rather, it is a healthy sign of self-assertion directed at mastering various challenges throughout the course of development. The distinction between the two basic types of aggressive behavior is obviously important when assessing the behavior of any child. Since Arthur's behavioral difficulties appear to stem more from withdrawal than aggression, and since his environment is supportive, he does not seem in danger of developing overly hostile aggressive tendencies of the type described by Parens.

On a theoretical level, the distinction between destructive and nondestructive aggression is useful for assessing behavior during Mahler's (Mahler, Pine, & Bergman, 1975) rapprochement subphase, a developmental phase when the infant is perhaps at highest risk for resorting to maladaptive aggression. During this period (18 to 24 months), the infant is struggling to establish a consistent identity while not only confronting and internalizing the threatening realization of being separate, but also trying to cope with three very primal fears: fear of object (mother) loss, fear of losing the object's love, and castration anxiety (Mahler et al., 1975).

Considering the great demands on the coping ability of the infant during this period, it is little wonder that the risk of developing destructive aggression is high. Significantly, McDevitt (1985) notes that the danger is not only one of outward-directed hostile aggression, but also of aggressive impulses directed inward. The emergence at this time of an early superego structure, when combined with the process of self-definition, may result in the shunting (repressing) of aggressive impulses into the unconscious, where they are represented in the form of fantasies. In some cases, the derivatives or residues of aggressive urges may be too potent to be repressed, resulting in overt self-destructive behavior or at the least depressed affect, oppositional accident proneness, or temper tantrums – or all four. Thus, the assessment that Arthur is not overly charged with aggressive urges gains further support from the fact that there is no history of accident-proneness or other self-destructive behaviors.

McDevitt also notes that on separation from the caregiver during the practicing subphase (10 to 15 months) the typically high levels of distress felt by the infant are often manifested as inner-directed anger, which contains an element of helpless rage. In a downward spiral of cause and effect, this rage, which may become manifest as passive withdrawal from the environment, carries a charge of anxious mood that further limits the infant's capacity to achieve a reasonable distance from the caregiver. Thus, the infant's ability to achieve self-object differentiation is further compromised during this period. This negative feedback dynamic can be highly pathologic and, as McDevitt points out, is most likely to be triggered by caregivers who neglect the child, prohibit any form of aggression, or behave in an overly interfering, intrusive, or controlling manner. While it is possible that Arthur experienced a level of frustration higher than the norm during the practicing subphase, due to his mother's intrusive attitude toward child-rearing, it seems unlikely that he was compromised so severely that he is in danger of psychopathology, since his performance deficit in school is only marginal.

This assessment is borne out by the fact that Arthur engages in few overt manifestations of incipient hostile aggression, which, according to McDevitt, include restriction of aim, traits of denial or avoidance, and turning on the self as manifested by the self-infliction of physical pain (e.g., pulling his or her own hair). Aggression may also be exhibited in the form of oppositional behavior or negativism, as expressed in provocations of the mother. However, by twelve months, normal object-directed aggressive behavior is generally mixed with playful or affectionate behavior—a phenomenon also noted by Parens (1979).

Development of Empathy

There is general agreement that the capacity to empathize with the potential recipient of an aggressive action serves as a major inhibitor of aggressive behavior (Staub, 1971). Therefore, the poor self-object differentiation inherent in an insecure attachment places the infant at risk not only of developing antisocial aggressive tendencies but also of failing to achieve proper inhibition of these destructive tendencies due to an inadequate ability to empathize with the moods, needs, and concerns of others.

An inadequate ability to form mental representations of self and others leads to impairment in differentiating between one's own intentions and those of others. Under these conditions, the child can only interpret the behavior of others—and the outcomes of those behaviors—in terms of his own intentions and subsequent physical events. For example, abused children might feel responsible for their own mistreatment if they confuse their emotions and intentions with those of their abusers. When the child harbors intentions of love toward the parents and in return receives harsh treatment, he may justify this to himself by rationalizing that he is being rightly punished. It is also possible that, with his peers, he may come to believe that aggressive behavior is a sign of affection and act accordingly. While Arthur seems in no danger of such gross misinterpretations, his ability to empathize should be assessed further, since his withdrawn behavior makes it easier for him to avoid interactions with others – a factor that could negatively influence empathic development.

Under the optimal circumstances of secure attachment, empathic ability has been reported in children as young as 18 months. Young toddlers of this age in a study by Zahn-Waxler and Radke-Yarrow (1982) were observed to offer comfort to distressed peers and family members. Some of these children even changed strategies if their initial attempts at consolation failed. Children of this age are only beginning to lose their egocentric viewpoint. Therefore, their struggle to understand the emotions of others demonstrates the great survival value of developing prosocial behaviors.

INFLUENCE OF TEMPERAMENT ON ATTACHMENT AND PROSOCIAL BEHAVIOR

Q: Do you like to play with your friends in the neighborhood?

A: Sure.

Q: Who do you like best, those friends or the ones in your school?

A: Jimmy and Sam! (the neighborhood friends)

Q: Why do you like them better?

A: 'Cause *they* like *me*!

The characteristics of the interaction between infant and mother are by no means restricted to the actions and reactions of the mother. The infant's innate degree of reactivity to environmental stimuli and constitutional level of self-reg-

ulatory ability make a significant contribution to the benefits derived from the attachment relationship (Derryberry &
Rothbart, 1984; Thomas et al., 1968). A high degree of reactivity to stress or novel stimuli, for example, may result in
diminished self-object differentiation, because this heightened sensitivity may cause the child to stay close to the
caregiver. This dynamic may explain Arthur's preference for
his neighborhood playmates and be indicative of frustrating,
aggression-inducing problems with self-object differentiation. Aside from being more familiar with (attached to) his
neighborhood pals, Arthur is able to stay closer to his mother than is the case when he is in school. In order to develop
along more beneficial prosocial lines, it is important that
Arthur remain in preschool long enough to forge new relationships in the absence of his mother. The resulting impairment in coping ability might be further exacerbated if the
child's temperament also included a component of self-regulatory inflexibility. This temperamental trait would make it
difficult for the child to shift out of the negative affect in-
duced by episodes of task failure.

That a child's temperamental disposition might interfere
with the acquisition of prosocial behavior is affirmed by the
observation that prosocial behavior is associated with positive affect, with conditions in which the child's needs are
being met, and with a state of overall emotionality (Chess &
Thomas, 1984; Hoffman, 1975; Strayer, 1980). A child who is
highly reactive to stress may become so aroused that he
leaves the scene of interaction, either by diverting his attention or through actually leaving, or acts out his or her frustration through overt hostile actions. In the first instance,
further acquisition of prosocial competencies will be hin-
dered; the latter instance carries with it the possibility that
antisocial behavior will become learned and engrained in behavior patterns.

Other observations about the interaction between temperament and prosocial behavior include the one by Battle
and Lacey (1972), Buss, Block, and Block (1980), and Victor,
Halverson, and Montague (1985) that highly active children

tend to participate in more frenetic play, frequently dominating their peers by sheer force of energy. Complementarily, Tischler (1980) has noted that very active children are disproportionately represented among the children who manifest self-destructive behavior. Since it is somewhat difficult to judge Arthur's activity level because of his posture of defensive withdrawal, it is possible that he is suppressing a good deal of his natural, inherent tendency to be energetic. If so, not only is he experiencing the stress of inhibiting his energetic tendencies, but he must also continue to regulate these tendencies in the face of domination by others who are no more energetic than he. If this dynamic exists, and if it continues, Arthur may be forced out of his mildly withdrawn state and into the world of action. In fact, this process may already be underway, as evidenced by his increased difficulties with playmates with whom he is familiar.

When discussing the influences of temperament on attachment and prosocial behavior, it is important to note, as Bowlby has, that a child with a difficult temperament can be transformed into a content, easy to manage toddler through sensitive, altruistic mothering. Similarly, an essentially easygoing infant can become an anxious, moody, and demanding toddler by insensitive or rejecting mothering. Thus, the modulating role of the mother appears to exert a somewhat greater influence than the innate temperament of the infant in terms of the acquisition of prosocial behavior and of nearly every other developmental milestone as well (Bowlby, 1988).

However, in the case of Arthur, with his prolonged failure to interact with new playmates at school, it is interesting to note the results of a study by Thompson and Lamb (1982), which emphasized the influence of temperament on stranger sociability. These investigators performed a short-term longitudinal study of the relationships among stranger sociability, temperament, and social experience in infants aged $12^{1}/_{2}$ and $19^{1}/_{2}$ months. In addition to confirming the finding of many investigators (e.g., Main, 1973) that a strong correlation exists between secure attachment and greater friendliness toward strangers, Thompson and Lamb (1982) found individual differences in stranger sociability to be strongly related to variations in temperament—especially fearfulness. Thus, it may be that Arthur's lack of sociability to his schoolmates receives a major portion of its impetus from his withdrawn, fearful temperament. On the other hand, if his withdrawal is due primarily to a possibly marginally insecure attachment relationship with his mother, further experience and interaction with peers will probably result in increased prosocial behavior.

The possibility of this eventuality occurring for Arthur receives further credence from a study by Lieberman (1977), who found that security of attachment was correlated predominantly with nonverbal measures of competence, such as collaboration in games, while peer experience was correlated largely with verbal measures. Since Arthur is an only child with a somewhat protective mother, his interactions with peers have probably been somewhat limited. Therefore, he may in fact be engaging with his new peers by the less obvious means of nonverbal cues—a process which might be a prelude to behavioral interaction.

EARLY EMERGENCE OF PROSOCIAL BEHAVIOR

Q: Arthur, do you like to help your friends when they have problems?
A: Uh-huh (nodding affirmatively).

Evolutionary Advantages of
Prosocial Behavior

Prosocial behavior is influenced by temperament and *mediated* by the relative security of the attachment bond, but it has its origins in a biologically based predisposition to help. As Hoffman (1982) has argued, the genetic fitness of an individual is measured not only by his individual genetic fitness and that of his offspring, but also by the enhancement of the fitness of other relatives who are members of the same gene pool. Therefore, natural selection favors genetic tendencies to perform altruistic acts when the recipients are closely enough related to the giver for a net increase in the giver's genes to result. This requisite *close* relationship need not be restricted to relatives; in fact, we humans all share genes. Eberhard (1975) has proven that the probability of altruistic behavior increases when (1) the beneficiary stands to gain a great deal (as in emergency situations); (2) the cost to the giver is low; (3) the donor is efficient at giving aid; and (4) the beneficiary is efficient at using the aid.

It is evident that altruism is a very plastic behavior with far-reaching survival value, especially when Trivers' (1971) notion of *reciprocal altruism* is brought into play. Reciprocal altruism is a uniquely human ability defined as the capacity to behave altruistically toward members of society who are totally unrelated to one's group, on the assumption that this altruism will be repaid in the future and thus contribute to the viability of one's genetic inheritance. Hoffman (1982) makes the valid point that survival requires altruism as well as egoism and therefore a behavioral disposition toward prosocial behavior must be built into the evolving human organism. He goes on to state that what was acquired through natural selection was actually a predisposition or motive to help. While still biologically based, our inherent prosociability is amenable to control by cognitive processes. Therefore, it was not altruistic action that was selected, but the *mediators* of altruistic action, providing humans with the necessary flexibility to judge whether or not a given altruistic act should be performed.

Verifying Prosocial Behavior in Preschoolers

If the urge to engage in altruistic acts has become inherent as a result of natural selection, this behavior should be manifested early in life, along with the other elements of emotional and cognitive development. While the study by Zahn-Waxler and Radke-Yarrow (1982) demonstrated empathic ability in 18-month-olds, much research remains to be done to reveal the early indicators of prosocial urges.

Denham (1986) corroborated and extended the findings of Zahn-Waxler and Radke-Yarrow in a carefully contextualized study of 27 two- and three-year-olds. Denham attempted to describe the affective perspective-taking abilities of these children, their prosocial behaviors in response to peer emotions, and the interrelation of these domains. She also examined the relationships between these variables and the emotions of the children.

In attempting study of these variables, Denham tried to overcome the measurement problems of prior studies. Among these were (1) overly restrictive operational definitions for prosocial behavior; (2) cognitively complex measures that were developmentally inappropriate; and (3) insufficient appreciation not only of the need to capture the attention of young children but also of embedding the tasks within an ongoing social context. She hypothesized that the previously sketchy evidence for a relationship between affective perspective-taking and prosocial behavior resulted from poor measurement systems. In addition, she attempted to take into account the fact that the basis of early prosocial reciprocity between young children is more likely to be the positive affect associated with mutually agreeable interchange than some kind of sophisticated cognitive processing.

Accordingly, Denham developed a contextualized system in which the children were exposed to a series of 14 vignettes enacted by puppets. In the affective perspective-taking condition, eight of the vignettes depicted the characters reacting normatively (e.g., fear during a nightmare). In the remaining six stories, the puppets reacted in a manner opposite to the way the child's mother reported the child would probably feel. Subjects were then asked to affix on the puppets one of four felt faces expressing happiness, sadness, anger, or fear.

In the cognitive perspective-taking condition, the puppets enacted five stories in which one character, arriving late, lacked privileged information about the actions of another puppet. Subjects were then asked to suppress their knowledge and show how the late-arriving puppet would respond (e.g., search for the red puppet at the red house instead of the blue house). The majority of children showed a non-egocentric inferential ability to perform both affective and cognitive perspective-taking under these highly contextualized, attention-getting conditions. In support of these findings, Watson (1981) demonstrated that by the age of three children can label a doll and discuss it as if it were an independent object, and by the age of four children can discuss their parents from the perspective of their behavioral role.

Denham stated that her results showed a strong correlation between empathy and prosocial behavior and supported theories relating the two, but at a much earlier age than had previously been believed. Thus, it appears that prosocial urges are indeed inherent and manifest themselves at an early age, along with developments in emotional and cognitive processing.

CONCLUSION

Q: (Arthur tugs at his mother's sleeve) Ma, can we go home now? I want to play with Jimmy and Sam.
A: Okay, Arthur. We'll go home.

Like all children, Arthur was endowed from birth with the urge to engage in prosocial behavior and with the ability to regulate that urge in a self-serving way. Superimposed on his regulatory abilities were his mother's regulation of his actions within the context of the attachment bond. In the best of all possible worlds, these two regulatory systems would complement each other, so that, given the opportunity to practice with siblings and peers, Arthur would develop an optimal level of prosocial skill. His primal prosocial urges would receive the modulation they need from a person with mature experience who is herself acting altruistically toward him.

Of course, Arthur doesn't live in the best of all possible worlds, and he has lacked the full range of prosocial advantages that accrue to someone who has ample opportunity to engage in social interaction with those of his own age without undue maternal intrusion. Nevertheless, Arthur's world is one that is "good enough" in terms of its ability to expose him to adaptive behaviors. His mother may have inhibited his growth somewhat by being overly attentive and causing him to feel hesitant about exploring the environment, but he is sufficiently emotionally and cognitively integrated so that, with practice in prosocial behavior, he is expected to correct his minor social deficits in a short time.

This case illustrates how exquisitely sensitive the preschooler is to the attachment relationship shared with the caregiver and how any disruptions in that relationship – such as the imminent birth of a new child – can disorganize the development of the child's prosocial behavior. As has been seen from this case history, Arthur's mother conveyed messages that were interpreted as being contradictory by the little boy. On the one hand, his mother appeared overly attentive and concerned with his well-being; yet, on the other hand, she was pregnant, a sign to Arthur that she might be abandoning him. Her behavior is particularly significant when one considers that Arthur has only recently achieved the developmental milestones of separation-individuation from his caregiver and has just started school.

The vulnerability of the child during the first year of preschool has not received enough attention in the literature. It should be remembered that preschool often represents the first time the child is expected to function independently of the caregiver and to forge prosocial bonds with others. In Arthur's case, however, the realization that his mother is pregnant and that, at least from his point of view, he may be "replaced" by a new baby may have aroused feelings of anxiety. If, after all, he cannot depend on his caregiver to offer him a secure relationship that is stable over time, how can he be expected to forge new relationships with the other children? Won't these friendships, like the bond he has established with his mother, be susceptible to change? This anxiety may lie at the root of Arthur's recent withdrawal from his classmates and quarrels with his friends.

Although there is no genuine psychopathology evident in this case, treatment will still be advantageous for both Arthur and his mother to help them realign feelings of security within the attachment relationships. Arthur must come to understand that a new baby in the family will not threaten his position or change the way in which his mother cares for him. It is only when the attachment bond between these two is reaffirmed that the child will experience sufficient affective security to venture forth into potential new relationships with friends at the preschool. Moreover, the treatment process should be designed to help not only Arthur but also his mother. She must become more aware of the significance of her actions for her son.

This case, then, serves as a paradigm demonstrating how variations – or what the child perceives to be variations – in the attachment relationship can affect the adaptive development of prosocial behaviors as the child begins to attend school for the first time. During this crucial period the caregiver must be particularly careful to maintain her supportive posture toward the child, so that separation anxiety, coupled with fear of loss of the mother, will not engulf the child, thwarting adaptive development.

7

AGGRESSIVE BEHAVIOR

JULIE

Julie, a petite, initially withdrawn three-and-a-half-year-old, was brought in by her parents, who were concerned about her behavior toward her baby brother, Sam. From the time Sam arrived in their home six months previously, Julie had engaged in a number of episodes of "rough handling" with him. Despite warnings and instructions on how to handle the baby, Julie persisted in playing roughly with Sam until, the day previous to her appearance at the clinic, she had succeeded in rolling him out of his bed and onto the floor.

As her parents discussed their concern, Julie first sat shyly on her mother's lap, where she was welcomed, and then moved to her father, who obligingly bounced her on his knee. This caused Julie to become very animated and full of gleeful laughter. The affection among the three family members was clear and genuine. It wasn't long before Julie dismounted from her father's leg and began an active exploration of the office.

"I just don't understand it," her mother said. "Julie was pretty destructive around the age of two, but that ended almost a year ago when I realized I should be at home with her and quit my job. She was fine before Sam arrived. At first, when she mishandled the baby I thought she was just being overenthusiastic and uncoordinated, but things keep happening."

When asked whether or not Julie had been disciplined in some way for her behavior, her mother responded that neither she nor Julie's father practiced corporal punishment. "We usually talk sternly to her," her father stated. "If she still doesn't behave we might deny her dessert or take one of her toys away."

Julie's father is a program executive at a local television station. Her mother is a freelance writer who works at home and "tries to give Julie as much stimulation" as she can. "I think the more a child is exposed to early on the brighter she'll be."

When asked about his activities with his daughter, Julie's father stated that he watched a good deal of television with her. "It's a good way to be with her and do some research of my own. Julie always asks a lot of questions, and seeing programs through her eyes is valuable to me. Plus, I hope I'm teaching her something by answering her questions."

At this point, Julie's mother said, "He has more patience than I do. He answers every one of her questions. She's very advanced for her age. Julie can already read the newspaper comics, and she doesn't like just to play games with other children very much."

Julie, who had been running her hands over a bookcase, accidently knocked a book to the floor and began to cry, looking worriedly at the adults. Her mother held out her arms and Julie came over for reassurance. When she quieted down, Julie was asked what she thought of her baby brother. "I like him," she said hesitantly. "I wish he could play more."

When asked if Julie was prone to getting into accidents, both parents agreed she was not. As her mother put it, "Julie is usually very careful about things. That's why I can't understand her treatment of Sam. Maybe it's just a brand-new experience and she doesn't know what to make of him."

AGGRESSION: A COMPLEX BEHAVIOR

This case raises one of the commonest issues confronting the parents of young children and clinicians who deal with this population. It involves sibling relationships, in particular, the rivalries that can erupt among siblings. It is known that a certain degree of sibling rivalry is part of the adaptive developmental process. Such rivalries are fairly easily explained when one considers that from the child's point of view any new entrant into the family presents a threat to his or her role as the key candidate of the parents' affection. Indeed, particularly between the ages of two and four years, when the child is just beginning to establish a firm sense of self and to negotiate the process of separation-individuation from the parents, the introduction of another child who will intrude upon the intimate rapport shared with the parents may be especially disruptive. When viewed from this perspective, however, a certain amount of sibling rivalry may be seen as adaptive. If the child becomes upset when a new infant is brought into the household, such distress indicates that the child does, in fact, share an adaptive relationship with the caregivers and is afraid that this relationship will be altered or changed by the entrance of the new sibling.

Although some degree of sibling rivalry may be normative, there are some types of behavior between siblings which are not normative. For example, excessive aggression, particularly when demonstrated in the form of physical assault against the sibling, may be a sign that the child is not adapting well to the new child into the household. In the case of Julie, there was some indication that this form of aggression was occurring, causing the clinician to posit that the little girl might be suffering from such *DSM-III-R* disorders as Attention Deficit Hyperactivity Disorder or Phase of Life Problem. The former disorder includes physically dangerous acts among its criteria for diagnosis, while the latter disorder involves a developmental disorder that arises as a result of the child going through a particular stage, such as separation from the parent. In Julie's case, as will be seen, the little girl's aggressive tendencies towards her younger brother were within the normal range. Nevertheless, when parents report instances of aggression by one sibling against another, the clinician must evaluate all phases of the child's development and determine whether such assertive actions arise from the naturally occurring jealousy triggered in the child who now has a rival for the parents' affections or have more profound origins that may be indicative of psychopathology.

Q: How are you feeling today? How do you feel when you wake up in the morning? Do you feel sad sometimes?
A: I'm fine. I don't feel sad.

The immediate cause for concern in Julie's case is whether or not she is engaging in inappropriate aggressive behavior. But we are also concerned with her mood, since in preschoolers, the etiology of aggression is very similar to that of depression, and the risk of later psychopathology associated with depression is well-known (Trad, 1986). When there is depressed affect in children there is also an increased likelihood of aggressive behavior. Depression occurs when children fail in their attempts to gain mastery and autonomy, and it is at these frustrating junctures that the child may act with hostile aggression in an effort to express rage and do away with an environmental structure that is defeating. Thus, as a part of assessing Julie's covertly aggressive actions toward her brother, it will be necessary to measure her affective state.

The close link between aggression and depression is further evidenced by the fact that both have been associated with loss and disordered attachments (Gaensbauer, 1980, 1982; Parke & Slaby, 1983); impulsiveness (Good, 1978; Gould, 1965); negative affect in parents (Frommer & O'Shea, 1973; Olweus, 1980a); temperament (Chess, 1970; Olweus, 1980b); and inadequate or disordered cognitive development (Dodge, 1980; Schowalter, 1970). The fact that all of these phenomena have, in turn, been identified as risk factors for suicide-like behavior strongly suggests that aggression and depression are powerful co-risk factors for aggressive behavior against the self, as well as for outward-directed aggression, even in young children (Trad, 1987).

The high frequency of aggressive behavior disturbances during childhood is reflected in the many aggression-related diagnoses listed in *DSM-III-R* that can apply to childhood:

(1) *Conduct Disorders* are characterized by a repetitive and persistent pattern of aggressive conduct in which the basic rights of others are violated, as manifested by either physical violence against persons or property, e.g., vandalism, rape, breaking and entering, firesetting, mugging, assault; or thefts outside the home involving confrontation with the victim (e.g., extortion, purse snatching, armed robbery).

(2) *Oppositional Disorder* manifests in the form of temper tantrums, argumentativeness, or provocative behavior.

(3) Unexplained rage reactions or self-mutilation (e.g., biting or hitting self, head banging are symptomatic for *Pervasive Developmental Disorder*.

(4) *Dysthymic Disorder* can be accompanied by irritable or excessive anger (in children expressed towards parents or caregivers) and by recurrent thoughts about death or suicide.

(5) *Major Depressive Episode* may carry recurrent thoughts about death, suicidal ideation, wishes to be dead, or attempts at suicide.

Aside from enhancing our understanding of the foregoing diagnoses, the study of aggression in children also promises to shed light on the nature of the severest form of dysregulated behavior: suicide and suicide-like activities. The basis for obtaining additional knowledge along this line lies in the fact that certain varieties of aggressive behavior have a strong heuristic component. The manifestations of aggressive behavior and its developmental trends can be charted and are thus more measurable than depression. Thus, the developmental analysis of aggressive behavior may provide behavioral clues for deviation toward self-destructive tendencies, particularly in the presence of depression.

The likelihood that such clues exist seems strong in light of the obvious relationship between pathological aggressive behavior and the inadequate coping that depressive disorders trigger in the individual. This relationship is intensified by the fact that aggressive behaviors, pathological or otherwise, appear to be very stable over time, as evidenced by the findings of Olweus (1979), who has performed the most extensive investigation of the stability of aggressive behavior to date. Reviewing 16 longitudinal studies, Olweus attempted to determine the degree of stability through correlation coefficients and found 24 such stability coefficients. The stability of aggressive behavior was found to be nearly as high as that of intelligence. This persistence of inappropriate aggressive behaviors may well result in depression after a sufficiently prolonged accumulation of ineffective aggressive actions. Such an accumulation would also be likely to produce elevated levels of frustration which, at the height of experienced displeasure, could conceivably generate an inwardly directed act of aggression (i.e., suicidal behavior).

The consistency of aggressive behavior also has implications in terms of predictive power, which is a major determinant of theoretical validity. Postulations based on longitudinal studies of aggression are likely to be valuable in light of the long-term stability of this behavior. However, in order to arrive at hypotheses which have predictive validity for longitudinal studies, it is first necessary to define the elements of personality whose psychopathological development could result in such behavior. Fundamentally, moderate or severe aggressive behavior that is inappropriate to the situation could result from strong feelings of insecurity or powerlessness or from an inadequately developed sense of empathy or guilt.

In terms of development, overwhelming feelings of insecurity are first manifested during the overlapping attachment and separation-individuation stages, around age two. From her mother's description, this may have been an especially difficult time for Julie. In terms of empathy, the evolution of cognition is one of the most salient developmental parameters. Here, Julie may be on firmer ground. In addition, models provided by the child's environment, such as parents, peers, and television, have the potential to produce misinterpretations of the severity of aggression necessary to achieve a goal. These factors will also be examined as they pertain to Julie.

The categories and relationships just mentioned are borne out by the fact that children displaying mostly negative emotions (e.g., sadness or anger) have been observed to have deficits in social-cognitive areas (Denham, 1986). This points to the necessity of achieving a clear understanding of social interactions prior to diagnosing such children. The social information-processing model of Dodge and co-workers (1986) promises to be particularly useful in this regard. Instead of attempting to reach a global definition of social competence (or incompetence; e.g., aggressive behavior), Dodge et al. have devised a means by which the relationship between cognitive skills and effective behavior can be uncovered in situation-specific instances.

While analysis of behavior in such specific situations as trying to obtain entry into a peer group promises to be very useful, the social contexts in which these various situations occur must also be considered. For this reason, an ecological approach to the study of aggression is recommended. The ecological model integrates different levels of individual development and different social contexts in an attempt to track the specifics of development over time. As Bronfenbrenner (1979) notes, "an ecological experiment is an effort to investigate the progressive accommodation between the growing human organism and its environmental systems or their structural component, with a careful attempt to control other sources of influence either by random assignment (planned experiment) or by matching (natural experiment)" (p. 36).

Therefore, assessing the continuities and discontinuities of behavior of an individual requires the integration of the sum of interactions between and among social, cultural, and physical factors and the individual. As Bronfenbrenner

(1979) points out, investigations have paid little attention to behavior in more than one setting. Nor has there been much attention directed to the way in which relations between settings affect the events occurring within them. This is all the more curious since it seems obvious that it is both practically and ethically infeasible to manipulate or control the primary variables associated with psychological growth within purely experimental contexts.

The inclusion of context in observations of behavioral learning necessitates recognition of reciprocity, the two-directional interaction between the individual and the environment. Further, the person is viewed not as a clean slate, but as a dynamic entity that progressively changes and causes change in the context in which it exists. This context, or environment, is more than a single limited setting. Many settings are recognized, as are the interconnections that exist between different settings.

In order to organize all these interactions, Bronfenbrenner (1977) and Brim (1959) propose an ecological environment whose topological arrangement consists of nested concentric structures, referred to as micro – and macrosystems. A microsystem consists of the complex of associations between a developing individual and the immediately surrounding environment, such as the home or school. A macrosystem describes a pattern within the culture at large, such as the economic or political system. A macrosystem is defined not only by its intrinsic structure but also by the information it carries. Such systems carry ideologies that motivate certain individuals and networks to behave and interrelate in particular ways. Analysis of these systems and their interactions among themselves and with the individual comprises the ecology of human development, which Bronfenbrenner (1977, p. 514) describes as,

> ... the scientific study of the progressive, mutual accommodation throughout the life span, between a growing human organism and the changing immediate environments in which it lives, as this process is

affected by relations obtaining within and between these immediate settings, as well as the larger social contexts, both formal and informal, in which the settings are embedded.

Thus, the ensuing issues regarding the development of aggression and its relationship to psychopathology during the preschool years will be examined in a reciprocal way, pertaining not only to single variables such as sex and temperament but also to major ecological structures and social settings.

PREDICTIVE VALIDITY

Q: Julie, do you ever argue with anyone when you're in school?
A: Sometimes.
Q: What happens when you get really mad at someone?
A: (shyly) I don't know.
Q: Did you ever kick anyone who made you mad?
A: (Julie's eyes widen) Nooo!

The degree to which outcome can be predicted is vital to the relative usefulness of any behavioral theory, and constructs of aggressive behavior are no exception. While the nature of the developmental process necessitates longitudinal research for assessing validity, it is still unknown if there is a particular period of development during which stability of behavior emerges.

Attempts to demonstrate conclusively long-lived effects from early crises such as prematurity or anoxia have not been successful (Drillen, 1964; Sameroff & Chandler, 1984; Weiner & Ader, 1965). Similarly, attempts to demonstrate long-term effects from later developmental events have been largely unsuccessful. For example, Magnusson, Stattin, and Allen (1985) studied the effects of puberty by following a cohort of 1,025 females from the early school years to adulthood. It was found that girls who mature relatively early tended to acquire friends who were older. One effect of having older friends was the introduction of alcohol into the activity patterns of the younger girls. However, the variable of frequency of drunkenness among early maturing girls failed to remain stable over time. Thus, the frequency with which young girls break social norms, at least for this variable, does not appear to predict later social maladaption.

Results such as those of Magnusson et al. (1985) bear out Rutter's (1987) observation that attention should be placed not on the changes associated with puberty or any other developmental milestone per se but on the different abilities and strategies used to cope with these changes. This is a useful suggestion. Since coping patterns evolve from early successful or unsuccessful attempts to negotiate developmental tasks such as self-representation, sufficient information relating to early development should make possible the prediction of developmental outcome.

This line of reasoning seems particularly plausible in the case of aggressive coping behavior. As mentioned, Olweus (1979), reviewing 16 longitudinal studies of aggression, found a high degree of stability to exist over time for this behavior. Several other investigators have reported a clear correlation between marked aggressiveness toward peers in the age range between eight and twelve years and later antisocial behavior (Farrington, 1978; Olweus, 1980a, 1980b; Robins, 1978).

In attempting to identify the variables that give rise to an aggressive reaction pattern, Olweus (1980a, 1980b) studied two samples of males. Sample one consisted of 76 boys between the ages of 12 and 14 years, along with their mothers and the majority of their fathers. The second sample was comprised of 51 boys between 15 and 17 years of age along with their mothers and 32 of their fathers. Peer ratings and parental interviews were used to assess four factors: (1) mother's negativism; (2) boy's temperament; (3) mother's permissiveness for aggression; and (4) parental use of powerful/assertive methods of discipline. Consonant with other reports, Olweus found a high correlation between the evolution of aggressive behavior patterns and three major variables: (1) highly negative mothers; (2) the use of physical punishment; and (3) the presence of a permissive attitude toward aggressive behavior. In terms of these variables, Julie appears to be at low risk for developing psychopathologic aggression.

However, when assessing the child's temperament as a discrete factor, Olweus not only found a correlation between a highly active, strident temperament and the development of aggression, but also provided evidence demonstrating the worth of temperament as a stable contributor to this behavior. Other researchers also have argued that temperament or perhaps clusters of temperamental traits are important in the development of aggression (e.g., Thomas & Chess, 1984). In the absence of a full evaluation of her temperament, this variable remains somewhat ambiguous in Julie's case, since her behavior seems neither highly active nor overtly withdrawn.

The ability to use certain elements in a child's makeup and environment to predict the subsequent development of an aggressive reaction pattern makes the study of aggression a promising and important enterprise. Not only will the clinician be able in some instances to identify and treat vulnerability to aggressive behavior, but related areas of psychopathology such as depression may also be detected. Furthermore, the demonstrated stability of aggressive behavior argues for the importance of isolating internal and external indicators and for early therapeutic intervention.

CAREGIVER-MEDIATED DEVELOPMENT OF AGGRESSIVE BEHAVIOR

Q: Do you think your mother is happy when you play when she's not around?
A: Um, yes.

Separation and Individuation

Feelings of insecurity in the infant occur naturally with the loss of egocentric outlook, the realization that she is dependent and separate rather than powerful and undifferentiated from the mother. However, the intensity of these feelings of loss can be exacerbated by inappropriate interactive caregiver behavior, such as neglect or overintrusive protectiveness. Elevated feelings of insecurity, particularly if the infant has a "fragile" temperament, may lead to the dysregulation of aggressive behavior (i.e., the consistent maladaptive use of aggression). This seems unlikely in Julie's case, since she feels her mother is supportive of her during playful excursions outside the context of their relationship.

Loss of egocentrism approximately parallels Mahler's (Mahler et al., 1975) "differentiation subphase" of separation and individuation from the caregiver, which roughly covers the period from five to ten months of age. While the infant is actively exploring during this period, the most distinctive affect displayed is that of "low-keyedness," which occurs most noticeably in the absence of the mother and is suggestive of a low-grade "anaclitic depression," a phenomenon first described by Spitz and Wolf in 1946.

During the practicing subphase, which occurs after differentiation, the infant continues to explore and to distance himself from the caregiver. However, during this subphase, the first deployment of autonomous behaviors, enhanced by the increased pleasure resulting from exploration, tends to offset any negative feelings the child may have in the absence of the caregiver (Mahler et al., 1975).

At approximately 16 months of age, following differentiation, the rapprochement subphase sets in. This is the most crucial stage in terms of the evolution of aggressive behavior. During the most acute portion of this period (18-20 to 24 months) the infant exhibits temper tantrums and other forms of extreme separation reactions. However, the particular behaviors are highly individual, being dependent upon the specifics of the mother-infant dyad. In general, aside from temper tantrums, the infant displays ambivalence about proximity to the caregiver, a tendency toward rapid mood swings, and dissatisfaction – all of which Julie displayed according to her mother's report.

Once the rapprochement subphase wanes, around age

three, the fourth and final stage of separation and individuation becomes dominant. Mahler et al. (1975) describe this as the "consolidation of individuality and the beginnings of emotional object constancy." This period is characterized by the attainment of not only a libidinal attachment to the love object but of an internal mental representation of that object.

Attachment

Before discussing the specifics of maladaptive aggressive behavior triggered by child-caregiver interactions, let us briefly review the dynamics of attachment, a developmental paradigm that is essentially analogous to that of separation and individuation.

Bowlby (1969) has defined a period of "maintenance and proximity to a discriminated figure by means of locomotion as well as signals" that occurs at approximately the same time as Mahler's practicing subphase (six months). During this period the infant begins to display a recognizable array of responses, such as following a departing mother and using her as a secure base as he or she begins to explore the environment. These actions indicate the ability to differentiate responses to mother, father, and others. Strangers are treated with growing caution and may get a response of vociferous alarm or withdrawal.

Bowlby identifies the next and final phase of attachment as the formation of a goal-corrected partnership, in which the child begins to make behavioral adjustments in order to maintain proximity. The caregiver is now seen as a separate object with predictable movements in time and space. With the realization that the mother has separate feelings and motives comes the urge to form a partnership, an urge which usually occurs sometime after the second year of life. At this point the dynamics of separation-individuation and attachment are very similar since, as Bowlby implies, the child cannot build a partnership until he or she becomes aware of separation from the mother.

Of the many behaviors involved in the attachment relationship, aggression is a key component. For example, during this period the infant experiences strong bursts of displeasure (i.e., insecurity) which he seeks to alleviate by aggressively demanding attention. Aggressive coping patterns can be highlighted by the strange situation, the investigational tool developed by Ainsworth and Wittig (1969) that aims to measure the degree of security with which the infant is attached to the caregiver.

Three basic patterns of infant behavioral responses are found to occur as measured by the strange situation. These include avoidant, securely attached, and resistant patterns. The avoidant infant displays very little desire to regain contact with the caregiver following separation. There is little distress when the mother leaves and the stranger is treated in much the same way as the mother. In contrast, securely attached infants are eager for contact with their mother when she returns and are able to exhibit a wide array of emotions, ranging from smiling to crying. Resistant infants are either very distressed or passive during the separations. In this regard, Julie appears to be at low risk for developing psychopathology, since her relationship to both parents appears to be very secure.

Relationship of Atypical
Separation-Individuation
and Aggression

The study of normative separation-individuation and attachment provides a point of comparison from which to examine the consequences of any abnormal dynamics there might be between the infant and his environment. At the outset it is useful to recall Parens' (1979) distinction between destructive and nondestructive aggression: Hostile/destructive aggression is directed at eliminating structure, and at its extreme requires the presence of "excessively felt displeasure"; nondestructive/nonhostile aggression is directed at mastering several challenges throughout development. The task at hand is to determine whether Julie is employing destructive or nondestructive aggression.

As McDevitt (1985) has pointed out, destructive aggressive behavior is most likely to be provoked by caregivers who neglect the child, prohibit any form of aggression, or who behave in an overly interfering, intrusive, anxious, or controlling manner. The child is left feeling angry, confused, insecure and ambivalent as a result of the inconsistent responses from the caregiver, because these interactions do not allow full autonomy and also do not permit the child to re-experience past feelings of omnipotence. While Julie's mother appears somewhat anxious and may overstimulate her daughter on occasion, it seems more likely that these factors contribute only minimally to Julie's behavior.

Relationship of Atypical
Attachment and Aggression

Psychopathology can also arise from insecurity deriving from a maladaptive attachment bond (e.g., resistant). As Main et al. (1985) have noted, attachment behaviors are the cumulative result of the entire history of infant-caregiver interaction and can be thought of as external manifestations of an internal working model of the self. Thus, the infant who is insecurely attached will have the disadvantage of trying to gain mastery over his or her environment using an unstable and thus maladaptive internal working representation of the self.

In the longitudinal study by Main et al., 40 children were tested in the "strange situation" as infants. Approximately one-third of them fell into the secure category; one-third were assessed to be insecure/avoidant; and one-third were insecure/disorganized/disoriented. When these children were six years old, the researchers visited their families in order to gain information regarding patterns of family interaction and child-rearing practices.

Interviews with the parents revealed that the parents of securely attached infants placed great value on attachment relationships, believing these relationships had a noticeable influence on personalities. Parents of insecurely attached infants, in contrast, placed minimal value on the relationship (avoidant infants), or were preoccupied with their own parents (ambivalent infants). The third set of parents had experienced the unresolved separation by death of an attachment figure prior to adulthood. This group was generally associated with infants displaying insecure/disorganized/disoriented attachment behavior.

Other studies corroborate the profound influence of the caregiver on the type of attachment. Radke-Yarrow et al. (1985) used a variation of the strange situation to study a group of 99 children whose mothers had either bipolar, unipolar, minor depression, or no history of affective disturbance. A high degree of maternal negative affect was found to correlate strongly with insecurely attached infants. These studies suggest that insecure attachments, with increased risk of anger/aggression, are often the consequence of maternal affective psychopathology – a risk factor not present in Julie's case.

Early Modulation of Aggression

As discussed, a number of investigators have argued that aggression emerges in the early years, even the early months, of life. Parens and McDevitt have argued that aggressive behavior coincides with Mahler's paradigm of separation-individuation, while Main, Radke-Yarrow, and others have reached similar conclusions using the analogous paradigm of the attachment bond. In both paradigms, the first three years of life are crucial to the development of aggression. But what are the principal modulators governing the type and degree of aggression to develop in a given child?

Aggressive behavior, for McDevitt, results when forceful prosecution of the libidinal aims observed during such ego pursuits as exploration, mastery, and coping is frustrated. McDevitt reported that hostile aggression, encompassing the aspect of anger, can be apparent during the age range from five to 36 months. Parens found the roots of aggression from birth on, particularly in unpleasure-related destructiveness, as inferred from rage in reaction to somatically painful stimuli. Parens also found evidence of nonaffective destructive discharges, as manifested by infant sucking activity and nondestructive aggression in persistent exploratory activity, activated in most cases from about three months of age (1979, p. 9). However, although Parens found aggressive activity in infants before five months, his observations are in accordance with McDevitt's in that he emphasized the striking biological upsurge in aggression from five months on, at the peak of symbiosis. Moreover, Parens states that at the end of symbiosis and the beginning of separation-individuation (six to twelve months), true hostility and hate begin to emerge in the infant's psyche, when sufficient self-object differentiation has been achieved.

Although these manifestations of aggression only intermittently appear at first, they slowly assume a pattern of recurring behavior for the child. By eight to ten months, McDevitt argues, the infant's distress at separation is marked, embodying an element of helpless rage. McDevitt emphasizes that the infant associates his or her distress with the absence of the mother but is unable to express anger directly to the mother during her absence. This may have been the case with Julie. With some infants, the anger appears to be inner-directed, experienced in the form of a passive, regressive withdrawal from the environment; this atypical affect has been labeled "low-keyedness." It is this unusual combination of distress and withdrawal that is reminiscent of "resistant" and "insecure-disorganized" infants in the strange situation paradigm. While Julie does not currently fit into either of these latter categories, her initially withdrawn behavior at the interview may have been an indicator of earlier difficulties arising from the absence of her mother—difficulties that have not been completely resolved.

Concerning the practicing subphase of separation-individuation, both Parens and McDevitt argue that nonhostile aggression (nondestructive discharge in Parens' terms) is a major determinant in successful separation and individuation. However, Parens observes how easily the frustration of strivings for autonomy at this time can mobilize hostile destructive impulses. Similarly, McDevitt notes that by nine months most infants sporadically hit, scratch, or kick with anger, but that this behavior is most pronounced in infants who are active temperamentally and in those whose mothers were frustrating, punitive, or unnecessarily stimulating.

These forms of defense are consistent with Parens' extensive research of normal development. Parens further notes that during the practicing subphase ambivalence emerges for the first time; in fact, he argues that the conflict of ambivalence energizes this subphase. Ambivalence here refers to the infant's mingled, coexisting feelings of love and hate toward the caregiver (or libidinal object). Parens emphasizes that the helplessness of the ego in this self-conflict can arouse two forms of aggression: (1) destructive impulses, possibly leading to rage; and (2) nondestructive aggression which fuels efforts at ego mastery (p. 185). Furthermore, Parens notes that it is during the practicing subphase, from the beginning of the second year on, that pleasurable discharges of destructiveness such as teasing and taunting, are first observed. Significantly, it is at this stage, with the first appearance of ambivalence, that the neutralization of destructiveness begins, fostered by the internalization of the admonitions of the caregiver (p. 217).

Like Parens, McDevitt also notes that the forceful activity of aggression during the practicing subphase can have a constructive aspect. For instance, by expressing his or her anger, the infant promotes distancing from the mother – and as a result, self-object differentiation. McDevitt found that excessive anger, in contrast to this constructive form of distancing, is often mixed with degrees of anxiety. He notes that this interaction, triggered by a caregiver who prohibits aggression, neglects the child, or is overly controlling, intrusive, or anxious, may evoke deviant forms of aggression. Furthermore, if the mother is ambivalent toward her child, she may misread the infant's behavioral clues and respond in an unpredictable manner. This may lead the child, who may wish to move away from the mother in order to explore and practice, to feel that he or she may not have a secure base to which to return. Such unpredictability confuses the child, encouraging either a form of precocious autonomy or an overtly dependent relationship. While Julie does not appear to be overly dependent, there does seem to be some indication of advanced or precocious personality organization. Again, this may be indicative of the difficulties experienced during the separation-individuation phase of development.

If the caregiver's ambivalence is sufficiently great or if the child is particularly fearful in temperament, a condition of learned helplessness may evolve, in addition to the possibility of premature ego formation (precocious autonomy). However, this is clearly not the case with Julie.

Both of these conditions may include a component of either inward – or outward-directed aggression, or both, since the child very likely feels rage at being thwarted in his attempts at exploration and autonomy. In one case reported by McDevitt, a child who experienced this indecision became less alert, poorly focused, showed minimal interest in people and things, and clung to the caregiver. During the tenth month, this child began to avoid looking back at his mother when exploring because the caregiver would inadvertently signal the child to return, causing confusion. In general, however, instead of being able to express his anger directly to his mother when she hampered his exploratory behavior, this child whined and fussed and had mild temper tantrums. In McDevitt's opinion, aggression in this case was expressed passively and turned inward. He noted that hostile aggression towards the mother must be expressed overtly during this period or else the infant will be frustrated in his efforts to achieve self-object differentiation and individuation. Excessive anger interferes with the infant's capacity to achieve a comfortable distancing and thus frustrates the process of self-object differentiation. During the practicing subphase, McDevitt found that these infants with tenuous caregiver relationships not only avoided and ignored their mothers, but also regressed from practicing to autoerotic and egocentric behaviors. These were particularly evident when caregivers were neglectful of their infants.

While the practicing subphase is important for the development of aggression in general, the most fragile period for the expression of hostile aggression is the rapprochement subphase, when the toddler becomes acutely cognizant of his or her separateness. As Mahler et al. describe, the rapprochement period is characterized by degrees of depression. The child's acute awareness of his or her separateness creates a heightened sense of the object. During this time, the infant will blatantly display jealousy if the caregiver shows interest in anyone or anything else. The child often feels angry, disappointed, and betrayed by a mother who neither permits full autonomy nor restores the child's former sense of omnipotence. His or her fears now embrace fear of loss of the object and loss of the object's love. As noted by both McDevitt and Parens, the aggressive impulses which the caregiver has disapproved of are now, as a consequence of the process of identification, equally disapproved of by the child's ego and superego precursors. These aggressive impulses are pushed into the realm of the unconscious, where they persist in the form of thoughts, fantasies, and wishes. If Julie still harbors destructive aggressive urges, the unconscious is almost surely where these feelings reside.

As McDevitt and Parens have both observed, a striking array of defense mechanisms emerge during the rapprochement subphase, while the child attempts to cope with destructive impulses. In this regard, neutralization plays a unique role, but because the ego's ability to neutralize develops slowly and is still incomplete at this stage, defense mechanisms are brought into play (Parens, 1979, p. 257). Among these defense mechanisms are discriminating ego identifications with maternal prohibitions, complex displacements and projections of aggression from the mother onto the animate and inanimate "non-mother" world, the splitting of object representation, along with repression and reaction formation that begin to emerge as a result of these conflicts.

During the rapprochement subphase, according to Parens, the upsurge of aggression experienced in the practicing subphase is somewhat lessened. By this time, the ego achieves its first degree of control over, and modulation of, the instinctual drives. Also during this subphase, the ego develops a widening capability to register and express affects, such as pride and shame reactions. According to Parens, aggression during this phase is determined largely by changes in the libido and the ego. Nonaffective and nondestructive trends in aggression play a secondary role, with hostile aggression—including pleasurable destructive discharge of aggression—playing a direct role in the vicissitudes of this subphase. Parens describes two factors of particular importance in terms of the arousal of unpleasure derived from hostile discharges: (1) a developmental factor that predisposes hostile destructiveness to be mobilized; and (2) a carryover of hostile destructiveness from the preexisting residual conflict of ambivalence that emerged during the practicing subphase. Julie may well fit into this scheme, since it is likely she harbors residual conflicts from an earlier time and may possess a temperament active or impulsive enough to mobilize her feelings about those conflicts.

Ambivalence, with its roots in the symbiosis phase, will be either ameliorated or intensified in the rapprochement phase. For instance, where a marked conflict of ambivalence exists, the valence of hostile destructiveness will be significantly greater. Moreover, the elation experienced by the infant in the practicing subphase is lowered in rapprochement due to the lessening of omnipotent feelings and excitement associated with the upsurge of aggression and the spurt of the sensorimotor organization of the ego and "the newly aroused libidinal need for the caregiver's love developed by the maturation of the ego and libido" (Parens, 1979, p. 381).

Under these conditions, the young child undertakes the rapprochement task of balancing ambivalent wishes to regress and remain fused with the symbiotic partner with a developmental need for separation and individuation. If the ego falls into a state of helplessness, feeling too much anxiety from this conflict, hostile/destructive impulses are mobilized. Here again, the role of the caregiver is primary in either allaying or intensifying these impulses. The maturation of libido during rapprochement is also essential, as a large segment of narcissistic libido becomes object libido. Without this development in the libido, Parens writes "civilizing the child would not proceed, at least as we know it" (p. 320). Moreover, it is the object libido that makes demands upon the ego to neutralize hostile aggression. Normal maturation of the psyche, according to Parens, consequently brings about other changes in the young ego, such as the emergence of empathy and altruism.

The ego's emerging capabilities also allow for an increased ability to delay the discharge during times of heightened unpleasure. This capability is often seen in pleasure-related discharges of hostile destructiveness, especially in the later emergence of scapegoating and prejudice – instances in which destructive impulses toward ambivalently loved objects (e.g., the caregiver) are displaced to lesser valued objects such as peers. These pleasure-related discharges of hostile aggressiveness become more elaborate with time (e.g., sibling rivalry and object-related jealousies). Here we have a very plausible explanation for Julie's behavior. Jealous of the time and attention her brother steals from her and perhaps of the fact that her mother is at home for her brother while she was not for Julie, Julie may well harbor some natural hostile aggressive impulses toward Sam.

Thus, in assessing the mediation of early aggressive tendencies, the most crucial issue appears to be one of frustration. That is, the child who is successful in achieving autonomy and in establishing a separate but mutually harmonious identity apart from the caregiver will not experience an excessive urge to perform hostile aggressive acts. On the other hand, the child whose efforts toward establishing autonomy are thwarted by an overly intrusive, interfering, or neglectful caregiver will feel frustrated, fearful, and unhappy. Such a child will not be able to resolve internal conflicts about the self and others and so will experience a strong urge to engage in hostile aggression—a coping mechanism which is primitive but nonetheless effective, in that it is intended to disrupt an unacceptable environment, thereby potentially setting the stage for something more manageable.

Both Parens and McDevitt conclude that the dynamics underlying the expression of hostile aggression involve a suboptimal environment, giving rise to an abnormal persistence into the rapprochement crisis of the naturally formed aggression of the practicing and differentiating subphases. Furthermore, as a consequence of these destructive urges, the rapprochement crisis will be exacerbated. Julie shows very minor signs of frustration and fearfulness (depression), possibly indicating some disturbances in her earlier attachment to her mother. However, Julie's affectionate relationship with both her mother and her father greatly mitigates the degree to which these factors contribute to overtly aggressive behavior.

MEDIATING ROLE OF BIOLOGICAL MAKEUP

Q: What do you do when somebody goes, "Boo!"?
A: (giggles) I scream!
Q: Do you ever cry when somebody scares you like that?
A: No.

Temperament

Before discussing complex etiology of aggressive behavior further, let us point out that the temperament of the child plays a major role in all developmental situations. In fact, the most profound influence in terms of the child's behavior most likely originates in the very nature of the child's dispositional tendencies (Olweus, 1980a, 1980b). Temperament, as defined by Derryberry and Rothbart (1984), consists of "constitutional differences in reactivity and self-regulation." Thus defined, it is not difficult to see that any reaction to environmental stimuli will be mediated by the particular temperamental makeup of the infant and/or child.

An example of the possible influence of temperament emerges from the observation that prosocial behavior correlates with positive affect, with conditions in which the child's needs are being met, and with overall emotionality (Chess & Thomas, 1984; Hoffman, 1975; Strayer, 1980). A child with a temperament highly reactive to stress may have such difficulty with some interactions that he or she either leaves or acts out his or her frustration throught hostility. Thus, learning in general and development of prosocial behavior in particular is curtailed.

Pertinent to this discussion is the evidence that children whose temperamental structure involves high levels of activity may be more predisposed to develop aggressive behaviors than their less active peers. For example, Buss et al. (1980) used teacher descriptions and mechanical actometers to assess the activity levels of 129 children at ages three and four. Data on personality characteristics were collected at ages three, four, and seven using the California Q Set. Children who were interpersonally very active were characterized as being more aggressive, less obedient, and more self-assertive. Other investigators have obtained similar results, reporting that highly active children take part in "more frenetic" play activities and tend to dominate their peers (Battle and Lacey, 1972; Victor et al., 1985). Also, in describing children who displayed self-destructive behavior, Tischler (1980) noted that many of the children who manifested self-destructive behavior were very active.

Sex

While the nature of sex differences relating to aggression is still being debated, the greater aggressiveness of boys has been widely acknowledged. In their extensive analysis of 32 studies, Maccoby and Jacklin (1980) found that this sex difference extends to verbal as well as physical aggression. The preponderance of male aggressive behavior was found to apply across cultures and in free-living primates as well. However, the direct cause of the greater male aggressiveness remains somewhat elusive. In the study by Maccoby and Jacklin, the sex difference did not appear to be an artifact of higher male activity levels or degrees of social interaction. Evidence for a possible hormonal contribution to the difference in aggressive behavior between the sexes is compelling in animals and is becoming so in humans. However, ambiguity remains regarding this issue. For example, Bandura (1965) performed a study in which children watched an actor (model) behaving aggressively on television. In one segment of the trial, the model received reinforcement for his aggressive actions while in the other segment he received no reinforcement. Bandura found that the introduction of positive incentives nearly eliminated the performance disparity between boys and girls. This result led Bandura to speculate that the sex differences in aggression may stem from differences in the willingness to exhibit aggressive responses rather than from differences in hormonal makeup.

This explanation has the advantage of not requiring a deficit in learning or a masculine role identification before aggression can emerge. However, the full explanation of sex differences in aggressive behavior will probably be ecologically rich, involving hormone-related differences in temperament as well as extensive interactions between many components of the micro – and macrosystems. For our purposes here, it is sufficient to say that the fact that Julie is a female somewhat lessens the probability of stridently aggressive behaviors.

COGNITIVE MEDIATION IN THE DEVELOPMENT OF AGGRESSION

Q: Does your brother Sam ever cry?
A: Yes.
Q: Why do you think he cries?

A: (assured) He's unhappy.
Q: What's he unhappy about, do you think?
A: He needs a diaper!
Q: What do you do when Sam needs a diaper?
A: I help mommy change him.

In the broadest sense, cognitive processes are vitally linked to the genesis of aggressive behavior, since inadequate cognitive development can, among other things, lead to low levels of goal achievement. The resulting frustration provides a fertile terrain for subsequent aggression directed either inward or outward.

In addition, White (1965) has posited an inhibitory role for cognition. For example, within this system, first-available responses to a stimulus can be inhibited when the operational rules of language become internalized, allowing further cognitive processing to take place. Aggressive children may partially lack this ability, relying too much on associative processing, which White describes as a system in which response is rapid, being dependent upon thinking patterns similar to those of animals in similar situations. This type of learning relies on conventional principles of association between stimulus and response.

In testing White's hypothesis, Camp (1977) studied 96 boys from 77 to 97 months of age. Forty-eight were rated aggressive on teacher rating scales, while 48 nonaggressive boys were used as matched controls. Camp found that aggressive young boys did rely predominantly on associative processing, which produced a rapid response style. It is important to note that there was no impairment of mediational ability in these children; rather, they exhibited a "production deficiency," a failure to use the mediational skills. Thus, aggressive children may not habitually apply "second thought" to their actions regarding either themselves or others. The fact that Julie is, if anything, cognitively advanced, strongly argues against a cognitive explanation for her possibly aggressive behavior.

The Development of Empathy

As mentioned earlier, researchers have generally agreed that the capacity to empathize with the recipient of an aggressive action serves as a major internal inhibitor of aggressive behavior (Staub, 1971). Without the capacity to differentiate their own intentions from those of others, aggressive children can only interpret the behavior of others (and the resultant outcomes) in terms of external physical events.

The capacity for empathy or affective perspective taking has been reported in children as young as 18 months who were observed to offer comfort to distressed peers and family members. Some of these infants even changed strategies and tried new strategies if their initial attempts failed (Zahn-Waxler & Radke-Yarrow, 1982). By her perception of a logical reason for Sam's distress and by her willingness to help, Julie demonstrates a capacity for affective perspective – taking – a good sign in terms of her ability to control aggressive urges.

While the positive reaction to the needs of others is described as active perspective-taking, the capabilities that give rise to this prosocial development are still in dispute. However, Feshbach (1979) suggests that there might be certain abilities requisite to the expression of empathy that are also correlates of prosocial behavior. These include affective perspective – taking, the ability to express a range of emotions (affective capacity), and affective responsiveness (the expression of emotions in general). Furthermore, Hoffman (1975) views developmental transformations of perspective-taking as forming the basis of empathy. It may be that, in Julie's case, her somewhat withdrawn attitude may be retarding her development in terms of perspective-taking and the learning of prosocial behaviors. This factor would serve as a disinhibitor of aggressive urges.

The results of Denham's (1986) study showing correlations between prosocial behavior and affective perspective-taking, emotionality, and prevalence of happy displays are strongly supportive of Feshbach's and Hoffman's theoretical views regarding empathy and prosocial behavior. As Denham notes, these relationships may be operating at an earlier age than previously assumed.

Attribution of Intent and Locus of Control

In order to more fully explore the ramifications of empathy in regard to aggressive behavior it will be helpful to elaborate on the previous discussion about the development of attribution of intent. If the ability to distinguish the intentions of oneself from the intentions of others is inadequate, a child might choose to duplicate violence inflicted on him or her by others because of confusion about both their own intentions and those of the aggressor. While this does not pertain to Julie's case, it does merit discussion.

The ability to properly attribute intent is necessary in order for children to form accurate mental representations of themselves and others in their environment. Implicit in these representations is the issue of perceived control. It has been argued that children tend to view the world as being predominantly externally controlled, due to their early dependence on others for both physical and emotional care (Curtis & Schildhaus, 1980). It would follow that as children grow away from egocentrism they would move from an assumption of external control to one of internal control.

Hegland & Galejs (1983), however, failed to find a linear relationship between lack of egocentrism and internal locus of control. Locus of control (LOC), egocentrism, and verbal skills were measured in 174 children between the ages of 37 and 78 months. While these researchers discovered a moderate correlation between perceived external locus of control and young age (first two years), no movement toward perceived internal LOC was noted in the third-year data. The authors note that these results might not have been obtained had the study been longitudinal or if the age range had been greater. Hegland and Galejs conclude that while many children do achieve a decentered social perspective which is reflected in a predominantly internal LOC by age four or five, many others do not develop an internal LOC. Interaction with other members of the child's social community apparently has a large impact on the development of locus of control.

The importance of internal versus external LOC in terms of aggression is illustrated in a study by Standahl (1975), who hypothesized that children with an internal LOC are most likely to employ verbal, symbolic mediators as a means of controlling their behavior. Children with an external LOC, on the other hand, will be uncertain of their ability to control external events. Therefore, they may be less likely to make an attempt at controlling their behavior through verbal or other means.

As was the case with the study by Hegland and Galejs (1983), the results obtained by Standahl were not clear-cut. Studies with juvenile delinquents, however, have demonstrated a preponderance of external LOC in these antisocial teenagers. Part of the problem in assessing LOC and its relationship to aggression in children may stem from confusions such as those cited in a study by Perry, Perry, Bussey, English, and Arnold (1980). Namely, if a child obeys an adult's instruction in the presence of a strong external pressure, such as a severe threat of punishment or a promised reward, he or she may be in doubt as to whether he or she acted in response to an internal belief or merely capitulated to outside pressure.

The task of comprehending causation and agency is further complicated by the concurrent development of empathic distress, which Hoffman (1982) defines as " . . . the involuntary, at times forceful experiencing of another person's painful emotional state. It may be elicited by expressive cues that directly express the other's feelings or by other cues that convey the impact of external events on him" (p. 613).

Cummings, Ianotti, and Zahn-Waxler (1985) observed the influence of the emotions of others on the aggressive behavior of 47 two-year-old children. During play, dyads of children familiar with each other were exposed to a sequence of background emotions of warmth and anger. The children developed distress in response to high levels of parental conflict and were more likely to act aggressively. Cummings speculated that arousal of distress may make children less able to tolerate frustration, which could then exacerbate aggressive behavior.

In a more direct approach to the effects of distress, Feshbach (1964) hypothesized that the consequences of an aggressive act should give rise to distress responses in an empathic observer even if the observer is the one who performed the aggressive act. This distress should then act as an inhibitor of further aggressive behavior. Thus, it would be expected that highly empathic children would engage in less aggressive behavior than those with lower empathic perception of distress.

In a later trial, Feshbach and Feshbach (1969) obtained data on 84 children in two age groups, a four-and five-year-old nursery-kindergarten group (n=48), and a group of children six to seven years old. The children individually observed pictures and heard affect-laden stories about children their own age. After the story, each child was asked to state how he/she felt. Subjects were then rated for empathy and aggression. Highly empathic boys in the older age group were, in fact, significantly less aggressive than those with lower empathic ability. However, the converse relationship held in the younger age group. That is, higher degrees of empathy in the four- and five-year-olds gave rise to higher levels of aggression. There were no significant differences between high and low empathy girls at either age level—a finding that demonstrates the frequently found difference in aggressive tendencies between males and females.

The result in the younger age group of boys is inconsistent with the hypothesis that highly empathic children are less aggressive. Feshbach and Feshbach explain that aggression is among many responses at the disposal of older children in social interactions, while younger children have a significantly more limited behavioral repertoire. Thus, the inverse relationship between empathic ability and aggression is more likely to be manifested in the older rather than the younger children. The relationship between empathy and aggression might contribute to Julie's overt expression of jealousy or hostility to her brother. Not having yet developed alternative means of expressing her displeasure, Julie may turn to primitive means of expressing dissatisfaction (e.g., aggression).

The fact that empathy can serve as a major regulator (i.e., inhibitor) of aggressive behavior again emphasizes the importance of cognition in the development of normative or psychopathologic aggressive behavior. Poor self-object representation (e.g., during a depressive episode) can lead to confusion about the emotions and intents of others, which in turn may produce a deficit in empathic ability. This deficit may then result in a reduced ability to inhibit aggressive urges.

Modulation of Intentionality

Just as aggression is modified by empathy via the capacity to differentiate intents, the learning of intentionality itself is modified by social interactions. Piaget (1926, 1927, 1929) originally found the very young child poorly equipped to learn from social situations, reporting that children in the preoperational stage of cognition were unable to distinguish between social and physical phenomena. Such psychological entities as thoughts, wishes, and dreams were often interpreted in physical terms (realism), whereas physical events might be seen as being caused by psychological events (artificialism). These results, however, have been contradicted by experiments using carefully contextualized settings. It is now known that children as young as three years are able to distinguish intended actions from mistakes, reflexes, and passive movements (Shultz, Wells, & Sarda, 1980).

There is, in fact, extensive evidence to show that by age three many children (including Julie) are quite capable of understanding the mechanisms behind behavioral and physical effects. By five years of age, children become aware that others are aware of the existence of intentions (recursive awareness of intent). Thus, they are able for the first time to voluntarily mask or disguise their own intentions if they wish (Shultz and Cloghesy, 1981).

By age five, children are also able to tell the difference between intending an action and intending a consequence of the action. In a longitudinal study, Shultz and Shamash (1981) observed 25 children at the ages of five, seven and nine years. In their paradigm, the child acting as the agent played a simple choose and match game opposing a mechanical gum ball machine which dispensed either red or green gum balls. The agent was instructed to choose either a red or a green gum ball in an attempt to match the color of the next ball to be released by the machine. The rule imposed was that if the colors matched, the agent would be able to keep both balls, but if they did not match, the machine would win both balls. The sequence of wins and losses varied randomly, as did the contravention of the agent's choice by the examiner, who occasionally insisted that the child select the color other than the one he had chosen. After each act, the examiner asked a question as to the intentional state of the agent ("Did you mean to play the green one?"). After each outcome, the examiner asked, "Did you mean to win/lose?"

By age five, not only were these children able to distinguish between intending an act and intending the consequence of an act, but they were also able to tell the difference between intended and unintended consequences. Assessment of the intentions of others were equivalent to assessments regarding their own intentions. Furthermore, previous experience with performing the act and expressing its consequences did not improve the ability to judge the intentions of others.

Despite the child's considerable ability to symbolically encode and store information, the majority of investigators have focused their attention strictly on observable manipulations of reinforcement to either the performer or the observer of aggressive actions. Perceived intent (the mental state responsible for guiding and organizing behavior) plays a key role in these investigations. Both children and adults tend to inhibit their aggressive responses when they believe a peer accidentally, and not intentionally, produced a negative outcome through aggression (Pastore, 1952; Rule, Nesdale, & McAra, 1974; Shantz & Voydanoff, 1973).

As Dodge (1980) observes, variations in cognitive development may result in variations in defensive aggressive behavior: "The 10-year-old child who persistently responds with aggression to a nonintentional negative outcome may be doing so because of a cue-utilization deficiency related to a lag in his ability to integrate information into his behavior" (p. 162). Alternatively, Dodge notes, such a child may not lack the ability to properly react to a cue but rather may distort the cue; i.e., he or she may engage in what Murray (1933) defined as complementary apperceptive projection, the process of inaccurately attributing intent along the lines of personal expectations. According to Murray, the incidence of misperceptions of this kind increases with the level of stimulus ambiguity. It might prove worthwhile to test Julie's reactions to ambiguous stimuli in this regard. However, her level of cognitive function does not indicate that this is a significant problem.

Dodge (1980) hypothesized that children who are inappropriately aggressive are most likely to incorrectly attribute a hostile intention to a peer when the intention of the peer's actions is ambiguous. To test this hypothesis Dodge presented aggressive and nonaggressive boys in grades two, four, and six with a negative outcome resulting from the behavior of a peer with either hostile, benign (accidental), or ambiguous intent. The results of this study demonstrated that both aggressive and nonaggressive boys in all three grades were capable of modulating their retaliatory behavior to a negative outcome in cases where the intention of the model was clearly understood to be benign. However, in the ambiguous condition, aggressive boys reacted with aggression, seemingly assuming hostile intent. As Dodge points out, these results do not support the idea that aggressive boys are unable to integrate intention cues into their behavior, since their behavior was different from the nonaggressive group only under the ambiguous condition.

Concerning regulating attribution of intent, it is important to recognize that a positive feedback system may evolve in situations where an aggressive child attributes hostile intentions under ambiguous circumstances. This negative assumption may serve to reinforce the aggressive child's view of his or her peers as hostile, thus leading to ever increasing levels of aggressive behavior, which may be difficult to change.

The various elements involved in modulating intentionality have recently been combined into a schema constructed by Dodge et al. (1986). Within the framework of this *social information processing model*, social behavior is regarded as being a function of the success with which a child processes a set of social environmental cues. The child is visualized as processing information in five sequential steps: (1) the encoding of social cues; (2) the mental representation of those cues; (3) accessing of potential behavioral responses; (4) evaluation and selection of an optimal response; and (5) enactment of the response. These steps are assumed to occur rapidly, frequently at a subconscious level. Each step must be considered in order for optimal decision-making. Inadequate processing can occur if the child neglects to consider a step (e.g., performing an action before evaluating its potential consequences). Alternatively, processing will also be deficient if the child reacts inaccurately or in a biased manner at any given step (e.g., misinterpreting a peer's cues).

These five steps are part of a cyclical relationship between social behavior and social information processing. First there is a social stimulus to which the child responds with the five steps. The outcome of these steps constitutes the child's social behavior, which then leads to judgments about the child by peers. Finally, these judgments influence the social behavior of the peers. Thus, in this system, any given social task provides the context for understanding social behavior. This is an important departure from previous definitions of "social competence," such as "judgment by another that an individual has behaved effectively" (McFall, 1982, p. 1). This and similar unclear descriptions "refer to separate constructs that may or may not empirically relate to each other" (Dodge et al., 1986, p. 1). Dodge and co-workers propose that, rather than trying to globally define social competence, it might be more useful to discover the way in which cognitive skills relate to more effective behavior.

In terms of the study of aggression, this model is useful in that it attempts to describe certain types of aggression as being clear indicators of social incompetence. For their initial purposes, Dodge and co-workers chose tasks of peer group entry and response to provocation by a peer. Two studies were performed. In the first, 43 children were chosen from kindergarten through second grade. Teachers and peers assessed these children in terms of being socially competent or incompetent. Children were then presented with videotaped stimuli designed to evaluate social information processing patterns in the singular domain of peer group entry. Next, each child was asked to participate in a real-life peer group entry task with two classroom peers.

In the second study, teacher nominations and peer interviews were again used to select 48 second-, third-, and fourth-grade children who were "severely aggressive and socially rejected." These were then matched with an equal number of teacher-nominated "nonaggressive and socially average" children. Children in this study were subjected to the peer group entry task as in study 1, but were also exposed to an actual provocation by a peer. Assessment of the five steps of social cue processing for both tasks was performed as in the first study.

As hypothesized, the characteristic patterns of information processing about peer group entry successfully predicted the degree to which these children were able to incorporate themselves into peer contexts. "Children who utilized presented cues (encoding step 1), who generated competent and nonaggressive strategies in response to a hypothetical entry situation (response search step 3), who evaluated incompetent responses negatively (response evaluation step 4), and who demonstrated high skill in enactment responses were relatively likely to perform competently and successfully in actual group entry behavior" (Dodge et al., 1986, p. 24).

Alternatively, children who fared poorly in gaining entry to peer groups were disruptive and engaged in nagging demands and incoherent behaviors, such as disagreeing with hosts without giving a reason. Thus, Dodge et al. conclude that the elements of social competence in this case include the establishment of a common ground with peers, negotiating and achieving positive reciprocity, and forestalling the occurrence of conflict. These findings confirm the proposition that the positive and negative reciprocity commonly seen in peer relations are meditated and perpetuated by children's social cognitions.

The results of the second study corroborated those obtained in the first regarding peer entry and further delineated the profile of the aggressive child in a confrontational situation. When provoked, such children are more likely to attribute hostile intent, to respond more quickly with aggression to the stimulus, and to interpret these aggressive responses in a positive light. These children were also found to be less successful in a peer entry task, using a higher proportion of disruptive entry tactics and showing less adaptive social behavior in the classroom and playground. It is interesting to note here that when Julie was asked about her brother's intentions; i.e., whether or not he "meant" to take her mother away from her sometimes, she responded "no" – guardedly. For a child this age, this is a perfectly normal response and does not indicate difficulty in attributing intent.

The plethora of patterns in social exchange revealed in these two studies points to the importance of using individual assessments of competence in the clinical setting. Dodge and co-workers have suggested adaptation of a three-step procedure for assessment of social competence used in a previous study by Dodge and Murphy (1984). First, the socially incompetent child must be identified, usually by relying upon the judgments of others. Second, those social situations in which the child's behavior is considered problematic must be identified. To do this, the source of referral may be interviewed or the child may be directly observed. Finally, the source of the social incompetence (within the child's five-step processing procedure of social cues) needs to be determined. Direct observation will help confirm whether the poor rating has an actual basis in behavior. If no such basis is visible, the clinician is then free to look for possible biases in the rater.

MEDIATION OF FAMILIAL INTERACTIONS: MAJOR ELEMENTS OF THE MICROSYSTEM

Q: Do your mother and father fight with each other or with you?
A: Sometimes.

While the social information processing model of Dodge et al. (1986) stresses the importance of analyzing specific behavioral situations in order to discover the relation of cognitive skills to social behavior, the ecological considerations of Bronfenbrenner (1979) illustrate the importance of considering these situations within the larger context of family and society. The largely internal factors of temperament, sex, cognition, and empathic ability are predominantly developed and refined within the microsystem of the family. For purposes of ecological evaluation of aggressive behavior, the family can be viewed as a network of interactive subsystems pertaining to generation, gender, and role.

The Family: An Arena for
Aggressive Behavior

In general, the preponderance of evidence indicates that motivation for prosocial behavior is sufficiently strong to result in more concordance than discordance among family members (Hartup, 1979). However, as Gelles and Straus (1979) point out, factors within the family can contribute to violent behavior. There are more events within the family over which disputes may develop. Intensity of interaction is higher than elsewhere, with family members presuming they have a right to attempt to influence one another. Also, families are insulated from the consequences of aggressive behavior because of the "right to privacy" extended by society to the family. Furthermore, due to the involuntary membership status of the child or social expectations imposed on adults, members of a family are less likely to leave a stressful situation. Finally, aggressive behavior can be facilitated by cultural norms that may condone the use of physical force within the family, although the same behavior would be proscribed if it occurred between non-relatives. The fact that Julie has expressed aggression only in the context of family argues well for her normative development.

Parent-Child Interactions

Investigations into parental influence on a child's aggressive behavior have centered primarily around child-rearing practices, although the way in which parents manage the home environment (setting territorial limits, scheduling meals, etc.) is coming under increased scrutiny (Clarke-Stewart, 1973). In regard to child-rearing practices, the effectiveness of punishment in controlling aggressive behavior is dependent upon such dimensions as timing, intensity, cognitive development, and the affective tenor of the parent-child relationship (Parke, 1970; Walters & Parke, 1967).

In a study of 90 boys between the ages of eight and ten years, Parke and Deur (1972) demonstrated the importance of another dimension in parental control of aggressive behavior: consistency of punishment. These investigators assessed the relative effectiveness of consistent and inconsistent punishment in controlling aggressive behavior. The boys were randomly assigned to one of five groups of 18 members each. Two groups received punishment 100% of the time and two more groups were manipulated on a 50%-punishment, 50%-nonreward schedule. Members of the fifth group were placed on an extinction schedule and received neither reward nor punishment for their punching behavior.

Overall, subjects in all punishment groups showed less persistence of aggressive behavior than subjects on the extinction schedule. Furthermore, consistent punishment produced significantly faster inhibition of aggression than inconsistent punishment. Interestingly, differences in the type of instructions that accompanied punishment ("you are playing the game badly" vs. "you will hear a bad noise") did not affect the subject's persistence.

The power of punishment consistency and the malleability of aggressive behavior is demonstrated in a study by Zahavi and Asher (1978). These investigators found that aggressive behavior decreased and positive behavior increased in children between three and five and a half years following simple verbal instruction from their teacher regarding the inefficacy of aggression and the benefits accruing from prosocial alternatives.

When parental punishment is inconsistent, aggressive behavior may be exaggerated, and in some cases to a great extent. Glueck and Glueck (1950) found patterns of inconsistent discipline throughout the histories of delinquent children. Such inconsistency occurred far less frequently in the parents nondelinquent children. Erratic disciplinary patterns have also been reported to be highly associated with criminality (McCord, McCord, & Howard, 1961).

Problems with differences across studies in the definition of inconsistent punishment led Deur and Parke (1970) to undertake a carefully designed study in which the differential effects on both resistance to extinction and resistance to continuous punishment of a trained aggressive hitting response were assessed with regard to four treatment conditions: continuous reward, intermittent reward, nonreward, and intermittent reward and punishment. Boys (n=120) ranging in age from 77 to 113 months were selected from two schools in upper-middle-class suburban residential neighborhoods. Six groups of 20 boys each were composed randomly and assigned to one of three acquisition schedules: 100% reward, 50% reward, and 50% punishment. After acquisition of the doll-hitting response, members of each group were assigned to one or two consequence conditions, extinction or continuous punishment.

In accordance with the later findings of Parke and Deur (1972), consistent punishment resulted in the fastest inhibition of aggressive behavior. Furthermore, Parke and Deur conclude that children receiving inconsistent punishment and reward for aggressive behavior will be more resistant to extinction of the behavior and will strongly resist consistently administered punishment.

One crucial aspect of punishment derives from the fact that inconsistency in discipline due to parental disagreement about child-rearing appears to be negatively associated with the development of ego control. The low degree of ego control found to be associated with parental disagreement may well contribute to an inability to suppress aggressive responses (Block, Block, & Morrison, 1981). It is important, however, to keep in mind that temperament strongly influences manifestations of aggressive behavior. In families where parents use physical punishment, low-aggressive children who identify strongly with their parents reportedly show little aggressive tendency. In contrast, punishment is positively correlated with aggression in high-aggressive children with moderate parental identification (Eron, Walder, & Lefkowitz, 1971). It is very clear—and fortunate—that virtually none of the parental risk factors for development of childhood aggression pertain to Julie. Not only do her parents agree about what modes of punishment to use and when to use them, but these punishments are nonphysical and are applied in a frugal and consistent manner.

Aside from the various contributions of temperament and parental disciplinary patterns, the affective environment surrounding the child can also influence the development of aggression. The degree of negative affect between parents has been seen to be directly related to the level of negative affect directed toward the infant or child (Peterson & Hartmann, 1977). Furthermore, negativity of the mother has been found to relate positively to the degree of depression in the child (Olweus, 1980a). In such conditions especially, a lax attitude of the parent concerning aggressive behavior will likely give rise to high levels of aggressive responding. Again, Julie escapes concern in terms of these factors.

There is no evidence to show that parental punishment alone, within normative limits, is responsible for subsequent aggressive behavior in children. However, Sears (1961) found that self-aggression was strongest in boys who had experienced severe frustrations and stringent control of their earliest outwardly aggressive acts. Thus, if the child is allowed a degree of latitude to express his aggressive urges, while at the same time being consistently punished in accordance with appropriate and reasonable rules, and if the home environment is managed with equal consistency, the chance of self-aggression resulting in suicide-like behavior will be significantly diminished.

Sibling Interactions

Violence among siblings appears to be the most prevalent form of intrafamily aggression (Parke & Slaby, 1983). Steinmetz (1977) studied 88 pairs of siblings from families with two or more children between the ages of 3 and 17. Specifically, 70% of the children used physical aggression to settle disputes, primarily over possessions, in families with children under eight years of age.

Not surprisingly, sex differences occur in nearly every study of sibling aggression. Straus and Hotaling (1980) found that the rate of aggression between siblings for boys with only brothers is more than twice that of boys with only sisters. This result led Straus and co-workers to conclude that the presence of females, in this case sisters, may inhibit aggression in boys.

While interactions among siblings may contain a high frequency of aggressive actions, in the majority of cases these actions do not appear to be the most salient feature of the relationship (Abramovitch, Corter, & Lando, 1979). Rivalry inevitably plays a role in sibling relationships, but the rewards of prosocial behavior are usually sufficient to provide a countervailing force. Furthermore, aggressive interactions between siblings are less likely to result in serious consequences than actions initiated by adults, since children rarely use extreme levels of aggression. Accordingly, there are higher rates of homicide between husband and wife and parent and child than between siblings (Parke & Slaby, 1983). If Julie is in fact being aggressive, her aggression is of a kind practiced in nearly every family at one time or another.

Interaction Among Peers

Moving concentrically outward from the family environment, the child encounters the school or nursery school environment. This setting, like home, must be assessed with the principle of reciprocity in mind – actions of the child tend to elicit similar actions from others in the environment and vice versa.

Peers encountered in the school setting or elsewhere carry on the modification and development of aggressive behavior begun in the home. Smith and Green (1975) observed the aggressive behaviors of children aged two and a half to five years in British educational institutions and found, in accordance with family studies, that boys were more frequently involved in aggressive activities than girls. Furthermore, a child aggressor who encountered no adult intervention was more likely to be successful in gaining the aim of his aggression than one who did encounter such intervention.

The preponderance of prosocial behavior over antisocial aggressive behavior found in families also seems to exist in the school setting, although age differences do begin to appear. Hartup and Coates (1967) studied 35 boys and 35 girls between the ages of three and four years, nine months. All subjects were enrolled in a laboratory preschool. These researchers found that four-year-olds engaged in significantly more positive social reinforcement than did the three-year-olds. Also, boys took part in more give-and-take play than did the girls, and younger girls bestowed much less affection and personal acceptance than boys and gave less total reinforcement. Interestingly, boys tended to reinforce boys and girls to reinforce girls.

The role of peers as reinforcing agents for each other is important in the development of aggressive behavior. Patterson, McNeal, and Hawkins (1967) found that an aggressor was more likely to repeat the aggressive act if the recipient of the behavior responded by withdrawing or crying. On the other hand, the behavior tended not to be repeated if the aggressive act was followed by retaliation, teacher intervention, or an attempt to recover property.

Thus, in general, the school/nursery provides the child with a chance to expand on what he or she has learned within the more limited setting of the family. Responses to aggressive behavior that were not effective in the home may prove adaptive in the expanded nursery setting with its broader behavioral base. Conversely, behaviors appropriate to family interactions may prove inadequate in the more rigorous impersonal setting of the school. However, the potential for developing psychopathological aggressive behavior within the school in the absence of antecedent problems in the family seems relatively remote.

THE INFLUENCE OF TELEVISION: A BRIDGE BETWEEN THE MICRO- AND MACROSYSTEMS

Q: Do you like to watch TV?
A: Yeah!
Q: What do you like to watch?
A: Cartoons!
Q: What's your favorite cartoon?
A: Ghostbusters.
Q: What do you like about Ghostbusters?

A: Slimer!
Q: Do you like to see the ghosts get shot and put away?
A: Yeah!
Q: Does your daddy watch Ghostbusters too?
A: (smiling happily) He always watches with me!

Shortly after the invention of television, concern was voiced from many quarters regarding the possibility that television might have the effect of increasing violent behavior in the viewer. In the beginning, television executives steadfastly maintained that there was no evidence to support this contention. However, research has since demonstrated that the early cause for concern may have had some justification, particularly with regard to children. Because children's cognitive capacities and experiential repertoires are not equivalent to those of an adult's, the question is raised as to the degree to which they may be susceptible to violence on the screen.

Part of the difficulty in making an assessment in young children stems from the fact that constructs of modeling phenomena are often heavily dependent on nonmediated associative mechanisms. The process of observational learning of behaviors such as aggression is typically presented as being one in which the behavior of the model elicits a similar behavior in the observer. Subsequently, these modeled actions become cues eliciting imitative responses. Hence, the occurrence of imitative or observational learning is often assumed to be contingent upon reinforcement of either the model or the observer.

As Bandura and Jeffery (1973) point out, this view has limited applicability in situations where the observer performs no response at the time of exposure – as is usually the case in watching television. In this circumstance, neither party may be reinforced, yet a response can be acquired, either days or weeks after the original behavior was modeled and in the absence of cuing from the model.

Thus, it is important to distinguish clearly between learning per se and performance, since reinforcement theories of imitation do not account for the learning of matching responses at times when the observer does not carry out the model's responses during the process of acquisition (Bandura, 1965). In order to explain the reproduction of a model's behavior when the model is absent, it is necessary to infer that the response patterns are stored in symbolic form within memory (Bandura & Jeffery, 1973).

Taking these issues into account, a contiguity theory of observational learning is often invoked to explain the acquisition of imitative responses in the absence of action performance or of reinforcers being given to either performer or observer (Sheffield, 1961). In this system, the sequence of responses demonstrated by the model evokes simultaneous sensory events in the observer. This contiguous association in the observer leads to the acquisition of perceptual and symbolic responses carrying cues that elicit a behavioral pattern corresponding to the motions that had been modeled.

Bandura, Ross, and Ross (1963) further suggest that contiguity may be the mechanism by which matching responses are acquired, whereas reinforcement of the model primarily affects the decision to perform or not perform the act. This conjecture seems reasonable in light of the fact that the matching rule, which children employ frequently to assess the intentions behind an action, is dependent upon the contiguity between information about an intentional state and the behavioral outcome of the action. The outcome is assessed to have been intended if the inferred intent matches the outcome.

The matching rule serves as a vital link between the processes of self-observation and observation of others because information about the intentional states can be obtained either on the basis of objectively available evidence or through subjective awareness, using the self as a referent (Shultz, 1982a). As an example of the difference between learning and performance and the use of the matching rule, the children in the trial by Bandura (1963) had observed aggressive acts that were punished and so failed to reproduce the model's action. However, several of these children were able to describe in detail the model's aggressive behavior after the experiment. Presumably, while they had not translated the model's responses into motor activity, they had nonetheless learned cognitive equivalents of those responses.

The findings of Bandura (1963) are very much in accord with studies of children's reactions to aggressive cartoons. Strong evidence has emerged showing that children are powerfully affected by the behavior of these caricatures. In fact, cartoon models may be as effective as those in real life with respect to eliciting aggressive behavior (Bandura et al., 1963). Not only is aggressive behavior increased, but tolerance of this behavior is increased as well (Thomas & Drabman, 1975).

Ellis and Sekyra (1972) studied 51 randomly selected first graders. During the pretreatment phase, children were observed for three days while measures of aggressive behavior were taken. The treatment phase consisted of exposure to one of two cartoon sequences. One sequence was very violent, depicting animated football players going through the process of hitting, tackling, fighting, and actually shooting the referee. The other sequence was neutral in terms of aggressive content, depicting a musical variety show.

Results showed that within the natural school environment violent cartoons produced a significant increase in post-viewing aggression. This increase was directly attributable to the cartoon's content and not to the viewing per se. Ellis and Sekyra point out that cartoons may provide especially dangerous television content because they not only condone but also facilitate antisocial behavior, since cartoon characters are rarely if ever punished for their behavior.

Eron (1963) studied a large group of third graders, obtaining information about television viewing habits from parents and about aggressive behavior from peers. Notably, there was a very strong positive correlation between the violence rating of favorite programs and the aggression of boys in the classroom. Eron also discussed research indicating that boys who watch more television are less aggressive than

boys who watch it less. This may be because television view-
ers are by temperament less active or perhaps they discharge their aggressive impulses through fantasy rather
than in their environment. It could also be that the time that
would be normally used in acting out aggression is taken up
by watching television. Eron also notes that boys who watch
more *violence* on television are apt to be more aggressive
than those who watch less. This could be the result of a
preference for violent programs or an attempt to increase
aggressive drive through aggressive viewing, or it could result from modeling of behavior after television characters.

The work by Bandura (1965) indicates that, while modeling may not be the sole cause, it does play an important role
in boosting aggressive behavior through television viewing.
He studied 66 children from 42 to 71 months old and found
that reinforcements administered to the model on the screen
resulted in the performance of matching responses. Bandura
found that response inhibition and disinhibition can be
transmitted vicariously through the observation of reinforcing consequences to a model's behavior. In addition, in the
absence of aversive consequences, antisocial behavior of the
model can result in disinhibition on a par with that seen to
occur with positive reinforcement.

Since the cognitive development of the young child is limited, his or her ability to understand a televised plot is compromised. The viewer must first differentially select the vital
pieces of information, ignoring extraneous detail. Then these
bits of information must be ordered according to a scheme.
Finally, the viewer needs to make certain inferences that
surpass what has actually occurred on the screen (Collins,
Wellman, Kensington, & Westby, 1978). The fact that children lack these skills to some extent places them at risk of
making judgments based more on emotion than cognition,
increasing the chance that they will misinterpret or ignore
negative consequences of aggressive behavior. Evidence indicates, however, that a competent adult co-viewer can greatly contribute to the proper interpretation of events and
thereby help curtail the development of inappropriate ag-

gressive behavior (Grusec, 1973). It is fortunate that Julie's father spends a good deal of time with her interpreting what she sees on television. If left to her own devices and allowed to choose violent programs, Julie might well experience an elevation in her aggressive urges.

The power of television to present models whose behavior strongly affects the behavior of children cannot be ignored, especially when disturbed children are involved. In addition, in the presence of depression, any increase in aggressive drive, whether through television viewing or other influences, has the potential to exacerbate self-destructive behavior.

CONCLUSION AND FINAL ASSESSMENT

The complexities inherent in the acquisition of aggressive behavior seem to yield best to a three-pronged investigative approach. First, the stability of this behavior over time — from six months into adolescence and beyond — argues strongly for the inclusion of attachment or separation/individuation phenomena in any attempt at comprehending etiology. In many respects, the capacity for social competence is profoundly influenced by the degree to which the early attempt to separate from the caregiver was successful. The predominating mood accompanying this attempt likely "casts the die," determining the developing individual's level of self-confidence, self-expectation, and concomitantly, the degree to which he or she evolves an effective cognitive world-representation and a sense of internal locus of control.

If the attachment bond is severely anxious or disordered, the individual may "learn" or come to believe even at the preverbal level that he or she is effectively helpless. Or, the child, reacting to undue caregiver ambivalence, may precociously form an identity that is ill-equipped to cope with later life developments. In either case, the child's attempts to gain autonomy and mastery produce frustration that can result in inward — or outward-directed acts of aggression.

Second, in addition to keeping in mind the possible effects

of perturbations in attachment or in the separation-individuation process, the clinician must make an effort to consider
factors relating to the child's temperament. Temperamentally active children are more predisposed to aggression, and
those who are highly reactive to stress may act aggressively
in order to escape what is to them an intolerable social
situation.

Finally, the interactive social context must be considered.
Family members, peers, and even the mass media play a
strong role in shaping, teaching, and modeling aggressive
behavior. They are also instrumental to the development of
cognition and empathy, the latter being one of the strongest
inhibitors of aggressive behavior.

Thus, the clinician has many factors to keep in mind when
attempting to detect and treat the contribution of inappropriate aggression to psychopathology. Although the observation of the child will both generate many possibilities and
rule out others, a focus on specific problems in well-defined
situations, as outlined by Dodge et al. (1986) may prove to be
the most fruitful approach to the assessment of the psychopathology of children's aggression.

In assessing the particular case of Julie, it must first be
remembered that no child develops perfectly or at an abso-
lutely steady rate. Overall, Julie displays normative development in terms of aggressive behavior. It is possible that she
is slightly depressed as a result of previous difficulties in
separating from her mother and this might be compromising
her ability to learn prosocial behaviors. The resultant impairment in the development of empathy may be allowing
conscious or unconscious urges toward her brother to become manifest.

These considerations notwithstanding, there are other
factors arguing for a normative level of aggressive activity –
principally that she expresses aggression only in the family
setting and does so toward a sibling and no one else. Being
three and a half, she has not yet developed alternative methods of expressing her displeasure.

With patience and understanding from her parents and

experience in the social setting of school, where she can quickly learn prosocial behaviors and develop a stronger sense of empathy, Julie is expected to develop very well.

In Julie's case, it was of critical importance to examine the degree to which she had achieved a coherent sense of self-identity during the separation-individuation phase of development. Assuming that the transition to an autonomous, self-sufficient personality had occurred adaptively, then the likelihood was good that the aggression Julie was manifesting towards her younger brother was attributable to residual feelings of jealousy that had arisen when her infant brother was brought home from the hospital. Such feelings would be perfectly understandable and in accord with the normative developmental processes, which indicate that some uncertainty about one's status within the family may represent the fact that the child believes his secure relationships with the parents will be threatened.

As was seen from the discussion on aggressive tendencies in young children, the origins of such destructive tendencies may be complex. Normal levels of aggression are adaptive and even necessary during certain periods of the developmental process—such as the period of rapprochement. In addition, a wide array of variables can influence the emergence of aggression, including the sex of the child, the child's age, status of cognitive and affective sophistication and family interaction. Each of these factors needs to be separately considered by the clinician before a determination is made about whether the child's aggression is within the normative range or is suggestive of patterns of abnormality. Moreover, the clinician should assess the child's specific experiences at the particular time the aggression emerges. In addition to looking at these factors, the clinician should ask whether there has been a recent geographic move in the family, whether the child is beginning a new school, or whether there has been a recent separation between parent and child.

In the case of Julie, further investigation revealed that her rapport with her parents was excellent. This was seen especially in observations of the child during therapeutic session. Affection between parents and child was open and appropriately demonstrable. Beyond this, Julie's father indicated that he and his daughter shared a rewarding relationship with respect to television viewing. The two often spoke about issues raised by the programs and Julie's father was eager to answer her questions.

REFERENCES

Abraham, K. G., & Christopherson, V. A. (1984). Perceived competence among rural middle school children: parental antecedents and relation to locus of control. *Journal of Early Adolescence, 4*(4), 343–351.

Abramovitch, R., Corter, C., & Lando, B. (1979). Sibling interaction in the home. *Child Development, 50*, 97–1003.

Abramson, L. Y., Seligman, M. E. P., & Teasdale, J. D. (1978). Learned helplessness in humans: Critique and reformulation. *Journal of Abnormal Psychology, 87*(1), 49–74.

Ainsworth, M. D. S. (1973). The development of infant-mother attachment. In B. M. Caldwell & H. N. Ricciuti (Eds.), *Review of child development research: Vol. 3.* Chicago: University of Chicago Press.

Ainsworth, M. D. S. (1979, April). *Attachment: Retrospect and prospect.* Presidential address at the meeting of the Society for Research in Child Development, San Francisco.

Ainsworth, M. D. S., & Bell, S. M. (1979). Attachment, exploration, and separation: Illustrated by the behavior of one-year-olds in a Strange Situation. *Child Development, 41*, 49–67.

Ainsworth, M. D. S., & Wittig, B. A. (1969). Attachment and exploration of one-year-olds in a strange situation. In B. M. Foss (Ed.), *Determinants of infant behavior. (Vol. 4).* London: Methuen.

American Psychiatric Association, (APA). (1987). *Diagnostic and statistical manual of mental disorders (3rd Ed., rev.), (DSM-III-R).* Washington, D.C.: American Psychiatric Association.

Anderson, C. R. (1977). Locus of control, coping behaviors and performance in a stress setting: A longitudinal study. *Journal of Applied Psychology, 62*, 446–451.

Anscombe, G. E. M. (1957). *Intention.* London: Blackwell.

Arend, R., Gove, F., & Sroufe, L. A. (1979). Continuity of individual adaptation from infancy to kindergarten: A reductive study of ego resilience and curiosity in preschoolers. *Child Development, 50*, 950–959.

Atkinson, J. W. (1964). *An introduction to motivation.* Princeton, NJ: Van Nostrand.

Baldwin, J. M. (1911). *Thought and things: Interest and art, or genetic epistemology, 3.* New York: Macmillan.

Bandura, A. (1963). Behavior therapy and identificatory learning. *American Journal of Orthopsychiatry, 33*, 591–601.

Bandura, A. (1965). Influence of model's reinforcement contingencies on the acquisition of imitative responses. *Journal of Personality and Social Psychology, 1*(6), 589–595.

Bandura, A., & Jeffery, R. W. (1973). Role of symbolic coding and rehearsal processes in observational learning. *Journal of Personality and Social Psychology, 26*(1), 122-130.

Bandura, A., Ross, D., & Ross, S. A. (1963). Imitation film-meditated aggression models. *Journal of Abnormal and Social Psychology, 66,* 3-11.

Baron-Cohen, S., Leslie, A. M., & Frith, U. (1986). Mechanical, behavioral and intentional understanding of picture stories in autistic children. *British Journal of Developmental Psychology, 4,* 113-125.

Bateson, G. (1956). The message "This is play." In B. Schanner (Ed.), *Group processes.* New York: Macy Foundation.

Battle, E., & Lacey, B. (1972). A context for hyperactivity in children over time. *Child Development, 43,* 757-773.

Battle, E. S. & Rotter, J. B. (1963). Children's feelings of personal control as related to social class and ethnic group. *Journal of Personality, 31*(4), 482-490.

Beck, A. T. (1963). Thinking and depression. *Archives of General Psychiatry, 9,* 324-333.

Beck, A. T. (1967). *Depression: clinical, experimental, and theoretical aspects.* New York: Hoeber.

Beck, A. T., Kovacs, M., & Weissman, A. (1979). Assessment of suicidal intention: the Scale for Suicide Ideation. *Journal of Consulting and Clinical Psychology* (Washington), *47,* 343-352.

Beck, A. T., Kovacs, M., & Weissman, A. (1975). Hopelessness and suicidal behavior. *JAMA, 234,* 1146-1149.

Beck, A. T., Steer, R. A., Kovacs, M., & Garrison, B. (1985). Hopelessness and eventual suicide: a 10-year prospective study of patients hospitalized with suicidal ideation. *American Journal of Psychiatry, 142,* 559-563.

Beck, A. T., Ward, C. H., & Mendelson, M. (1961). An inventory for measuring depression. *Archives of General Psychiatry, 4,* 561-571.

Beck, A. T., Ward, C. H., Lester, D., et al. (1974). The measurement of pessimism: The Hopelessness Scale. *Journal of Consulting Clinical Psychology, 42,* 861-865.

Berkowitz, L., & Alioto, J. T. (1973). The meaning of an observed event. *Journal of Personality and Social Psychology, 28,* 206-217.

Bigelow, R. (1972). The evolution of cooperation, aggression, and self-control. *Nebraska Symposium on Motivation, 20,* 1-57.

Bigner, J. J. (1974). Second born's discrimination of sibling role concepts. *Development Psychology, 10,* 564-573.

Bladow, L. (1982). Locus of control of learning disabled and nondisabled children. *Psychological Reports, 50,* 1310.

Block, J. (1950). An experimental investigation of the construct of ego-control. *Unpublished doctoral dissertation,* Stanford University.

Block, J. H. (1951). An experimental study of a topological representation of ego structure. *Unpublished doctoral dissertation,* Stanford University.

Block, J. H., & Block, J. (1980). The role of ego-control and ego-resiliency in the organization of behavior. In W. Andrew Collins (Ed.) *Development of Cognition, Affect, and Social Relations. The Minnesota Symposia on Child Psychology: Vol. 13* (pp. 39-101). Hillsdale, NJ: Lawrence Erlbaum.

Block, J. H., Block, J., & Morrison, A. (1981). Parental agreement-disagreement on child-rearing orientations and gender-related personality correlates in children. *Child Development, 52,* 965-974.

Bowlby, J. (1960). Grief and mourning in infancy and early childhood. *Psychoanalytic Study of the Child, 15,* 9-52.

Bowlby, J. (1969). *Attachment and loss: Vol. 1. Attachment.* London: Hogarth.

Bowlby, J. (1973). *Attachment and loss, Vol. 2: Separation: Anxiety and anger.* New York: Basic Books.

Bowlby, J. (1980). *Attachment and loss: Vol. 3. Loss.* New York: Basic Books.

Bowlby, J. (1982). Attachment and loss: Retrospect and prospect. *American Journal of Orthopsychiatry, 52,* 664-678.

Bowlby, J. (1983). *Attachment and Loss. Vol. 1. Attachment (2nd Ed.)* New York: Basic Books.

Bowlby, J. (1988). Developmental psychiatry comes of age. *American Journal of Psychiatry, 145*(1), 1-10.

Brazelton, T. B., Koslowski, B., & Main, M. (1974). The origins of reciprocity: The early mother-infant interaction. In M. Lewis & L. A. Rosenblum (Eds.), *The effect of the infant on its caregiver* (pp. 49-76). New York: Wiley.

Brehm, J. (1966). *A theory of psychological reactance.* New York: Academic Press.

Brim, O. G. (1959). *Education for child rearing.* New York: Russell Sage Foundation.

Bronfenbrenner, U. (1977). Toward an experimental ecology of human development. *American Journal of Psychology, 32,* 513-529.

Bronfenbrenner, U. (1979). *The ecology of human development: Experiments by nature and design.* Cambridge, MA: Harvard University Press.

Brophy, J. E., & Good, T. L. (1974). *Teacher-student relationships: Causes and consequences.* New York: Holt, Rhinehart, & Winston.

Bruner, J. S. (1972). Nature and uses of immaturity. *American Psychologist, 27,* 687-708.

Bullock, M., & Gelman, R. (1979). Preschool children's assumptions about cause and effect: Temporal ordering. *Child Development, 50*(1), 89-96.

Buss, A. H., & Plomin, R. (1975). *A temperamental theory of personality.* New York: Wiley.

Buss, D. M., Block, J. H., & Block, J. (1980). Preschool activity level: Personality correlates and developmental implications. *Child Development, 51,* 401-408.

Camp, B. W. (1977). Verbal meditation in young aggressive boys. *Journal of Abnormal Psychology, 86*(2), 145-153.

Cassidy, J. (1988). Child-mother attachment and the self in six-year-olds. *Child Development, 59,* 121-134.

Chambers, J. C., & Tavuchis, N. (1976). Kids and kin: Children's understanding of American kin terms. *Journal of Child Language, 3,* 63-80.

Chess, S. (1970). Temperament and children at risk. In E. J. Anthony & C. Koupernik (Eds.), *The Child and His Family* (pp. 121-130). New York: Wiley Interscience.

Chess, S., & Thomas, A. (1984). *Origins and evolution of behavior disorders: From infancy to early adult life.* New York: Brunner/Mazel.

Chess, T. A., Birch H. G., Hertzig, M. E., & Korn, S. (1963). *Behavior individuality in early childhood.* New York: New York University Press.

Cicchetti, D. (1984). The emergence of developmental psychopathology. *Child Development, 55,* 1–7.

Clarke-Stewart, K. A. (1973). Interactions between mothers and their young children: Characteristics and consequences. *Monographs of the Society for Research in Child Development, 38,* 5–6.

Collins, W. A., Wellman, H., Kensington, A. H., & Westby, S. D. (1978). Age-related aspects of comprehension and inference from a televised dramatic narrative. *Child Development, 49,* 389–399.

Corsaro, W. (1979). Young children's conception of status and role. *Sociology of Education, 52,* 46–59.

Crandall, J. E. (1967). Familiarity, preference, and expectancy arousal. *Journal of Experimental Psychology, 73*(3), 374–381.

Cummings, E. M., Ianotti, R. J., & Zahn-Waxler, C. (1985). Influence of conflict between adults in the emotions and aggression of young children. *Developmental Psychology, 21*(3), 495–507.

Curtis, R. C., & Schildhaus, J. (1980). Children's attributions to self and situation. *The Journal of Social Psychiatry, 110,* 109–114.

Davidson, J. W. (1975). Locus-of-control and observed dependency behavior in a group of day care center subjects. *DAI, 36*(6), Sec B, 3118.

DeCasper, A. J., & Carstens, A. A. (1981). Contingencies of stimulation: effects on learning and emotion in neonates. *Infant Behavior and Development, 4,* 19–35.

Denham, S. A. (1986). Social cognition, prosocial behavior, and emotion in preschoolers: contextual validation. *Child Development, 57,* 194–201.

Denney, D. R., & Frisch, M. B. (1981). The role of neuroticism in relation to life stress and illness. *Journal of Psychosomatic Research, 25*(4), 303–307.

Derryberry, D., & Rothbart, M. K. (1984). Emotion, attention, and temperament. In C. E. Izard, J. Kagan, & R. B. Zajonc (Eds.), *Emotions, cognition and behavior* (pp. 132–166). Cambridge, England: Cambridge University Press.

Deur, J. L., & Parke, R. D. (1970). The effects of inconsistent punishment. *Developmental Psychology, 2,* 403–411.

Dodge, K. A. (1980). Social cognition and children's aggressive behavior. *Child Development, 51,* 162–170.

Dodge, K. A., & Murphy, R. R. (1984). The assessment of social competence in adolescents. In P. Karoly & J. J. Steffen (Eds.), *Advances in child behavioral analysis and therapy: Vol. 4. Adolescent behavior disorders: Current perspectives* (pp. 61–96). Lexington, MA: Heath.

Dodge, K. A., Pettit, G. S., McClaskey, C. L., & Brown, M. M. (1986). Social Competence in Children. *Monographs of the Society for Research in Child Development, 51*(2, Serial No. 213).

Donaldson, M. (1978). *Children's minds.* New York: Norton.

Drillen, C. M. (1964). *The growth and development of the prematurely born infant.* Baltimore: Williams & Wilkins.

Dudley-Marling, C. C., Snider, V., & Tarver, S. G. (1982). Locus of control and learning disabilities: a review and discussion. *Perceptual and Motor Skills, 54,* 503-514.

Dweck, C. S. (1975). The role of expectations and attributions in the alleviation of learned helplessness. *Journal of Personality and Social Psychology, 31*(4), 674-685.

Dweck, C. S., & Elliot, E. S. (1983). Achievement motivation. In P. H. Mussen (series Ed.), E. M. Hetherington (Ed.), *Handbook of Child Psychology, 4th Ed., Socialization, personality, and social development.* New York: Wiley and Sons.

Dweck, C. S., & Reppuci, N. D. (1973). Learned helplessness and reinforcement responsibility in children. *Journal of Personality and Social Psychology, 38,* 441-452.

Dyer, J. A. T., & Kreitman N. (1984). Hopelessness, depression, and suicidal intent in parasuicide. *British Journal of Psychiatry, 144,* 127 133.

Eberhard, M. J. (1975). The evolution of social behavior by kin selection. *Quarterly Review of Biology, 50,* 1-33.

Elder, J., & Pederson, R. (1978). Preschool children's use of objects in symbolic play. *Child Development, 49,* 33-47.

Elkind, D. (1962). Children's conception of brother and sister: Piaget Replication Study V. *Journal of Genetic Psychology, 100,* 129-136.

Elkind, D. (1976). Cognitive development and psychopathology: Observation on egocentrism and ego defense. In R. Schopler (Ed.), *Psychopathology and child development.* New York: Plenum Press.

Ellis, G. T., & Sekyra, E. (1972). The effect of aggressive cartoons. *Journal of Psychology, 81,* 37-43.

Ellis, R. H., & Milner, J. S. (1981). Child abuse and locus of control. *Psychological Reports, 48,* 507-510.

Emmerich, W. (1959). Young children's discriminations of parent and child roles. *Child Development, 30,* 403-419.

Emmerich, W. (1961). Family role concepts of children age six to ten. *Child Development, 32,* 609-624.

Eron, L. D. (1963). Relationship of TV viewing habits and aggressive behavior in children. *Journal of Abnormal and Social Psychology, 67*(2), 193-196.

Eron, L. D., Walder, L. O., & Lefkowitz, M. M. (1971). *Learning aggression in children.* Boston: Little, Brown & Company.

Farrington, D. P. (1978). The family backgrounds of aggressive youths. In L. A. Hersov, M. Berger, & D. Shaffer (Eds.), *Aggression and antisocial behavior in childhood and adolescence.* Oxford, England: Pergamon Press.

Fein, G. (1979). Echoes from the nursery: Piaget, Vygotsky, and the relationship between language and play. *New Directions for Child Development, 6,* 1-14.

Fein, G. (1981). Pretend play in childhood: An integrative review. *Child Development, 52,* 1095-1118.

Feiring, C., & Lewis, M. (1978). The child as a member of the family system. *Behavioral Science, 23,* 225-233.

Fenson, L., Kagan, J., Kearsley, R. B., & Zelazo, P. R. (1976). The developmental progression of manipulative play in the first two years. *Child Development, 47,* 232-236.

Feshbach, N. (1979). Studies of emphatic behavior in children. In B. Maher (Ed.), *Progress in experimental personality research. Vol. 8* (pp. 1–45). New York: Academic Press.

Feshbach, N. D., & Feshbach, S. (1969). The relationship between empathy and aggression in two age groups. *Developmental Psychology, 1,* 102–107.

Feshbach, S. (1964). The function of aggression. *Psychological Review, 71,* 257–272.

Findley, M. J., & Cooper, H. M. (1983). Locus of control and academic achievement: a literature review. *Journal of Personality and Social Psychology, 44,* 419–427.

Fink, R. S. (1976). Imaginative play in cognitive development. *Psychological Reports, 39,* 895–906.

Fink, R. S. (1981). Role of imaginative play in cognitive development. *Psychological Reports, 39*(3, Pt. 1), 895–906.

Fischer, M., Rolf, J. E., Hasazi, J. E., Cummings, L. (1984). Follow-up of a preschool epidemiological sample: cross-age continuities and predictions of later adjustment with internalizing and externalizing dimensions of behavior. *Child Development, 55,* 137–150.

Flavell, J. H. (1963). *The developmental psychology of Jean Piaget.* Princeton, NJ: Van Nostrand.

Flavell, J. H., Flavell, E. R., & Green, F. L. (1983). Development of the appearance-reality distinction. *Cognitive Psychology, 15,* 95–120.

Flavell, J. H., Green, F. L., & Flavell, E. R. (1986). Development of knowledge about the appearance-reality distinction. *Monographs of the Society for Research in Child Development, 51*(1), 55–65.

Frankl, L. (1963). Self-preservation and the development of accident-proneness in children and adolescents. *Psychoanalytic Study of the Child, 18,* 464–483.

Franklin, R. D. (1963). Youth's expectancies about internal versus external control of reinforcement related to N variables. *Dissertation Abstracts, 24*(4), 1684.

Freedman, J. L., Carlsmith, J. M., & Sears, D. O. (1974). *Social psychology.* Englewood Cliffs, NJ: Prentice Hall.

Freud, S. (1909). Analysis of a phobia in a five-year-old boy. In J. Strachey (Ed. & Trans.), *Standard Edition of the Complete Works of Sigmund Freud (Vol. 10).* New York: Norton.

Freud, S. (1922). *Beyond the pleasure principle.* London: International Psycho-Analytical Press. (C. J. M. Hubback, Trans.).

Freud, S. (1932). The ego and the id. In J. Strachey (Ed. and trans.), *Standard Edition of the Complete Psychological Works of Sigmund Freud (Vol. 19).* New York: Norton.

Frommer, E. A., & O'Shea, G. (1973). Importance of childhood experience in relation to problems of marriage and family building. *British Journal of Psychiatry, 123*(57), 157–160.

Gaensbauer, T. J. (1980). Anaclitic depression in a 3½-month-old child. *American Journal of Psychiatry, 137*(7), 841–842.

Gaensbauer, T. J. (1982). The differentiation of discrete affects – A case report. *Psychoanalytic Study of the Child, 37,* 29–66.

Galejs, I., & Hegland, S. (1982). Locus of control and task persistence in preschool children. *Journal of Social Psychology, 117*(2), 227–231.

Garber, J., Miller, S. M., & Abramson, L. Y. (1980). On the distinction between anxiety and depression: Perceived control, certainty and the probablity of goal attainment. In J. Garber & M. E. P. Seligman (Eds.), *Human helplessness: Theory and applications.* New York: Academic Press.

Gatchel, R. J. (1980). Perceived control: A review and evaluation of therapeutic implications. In A. Baum & J. E. Singer (Eds.), *Advances in environmental psychology: Vol. 2. Applications of personal control.* Hillsdale, NJ: Erlbaum.

Gelles, R. J., & Straus, M. A. (1979). Determinants of violence in the family: Toward a theoretical integration. In W. R. Burr, R. Hill, F. I. Nye (Eds.), *Contemporary theories about the family (Vol. 1)* (pp. 549–581). New York: Free Press.

Germain, R. B. (1985). Beyond the internal-external continuum: the development of formal operational reasoning about control of reinforcements. *Adolescence, 20*(80), 939–947.

Gershowitz, M. (1974). Fantasy behaviors of clinic-referred children in play environments with college undergraduates. *Unpublished Doctoral dissertation,* Michigan State University.

Glueck, S., & Glueck, E. (1950). *Unraveling juvenile delinquency.* New York: Commonwealth Fund.

Goldney, R. D. (1982). Locus of control in young women who have attempted suicide. *The Journal of Nervous and Mental Disease, 170*(4), 198–201.

Goldney, R. D. (1985). Parental representation in young women who attempt suicide. *Acta Psychiatrica Scandinavica, 72,* 230–232.

Goldschmidt, M. L., & Bentler, P. M. (1968). Dimensions and measurement of conversation. *Child Development, 39,* 787–802.

Golomb, C., & Cornelius, C. B. (1977). Symbolic play and its cognitive significance. *Developmental Psychology, 13,* 246–252.

Good, L. I. (1987). Reference to reality, social context, and gender as sources of variation in perceived models of social behavior. *Dissertation Abstracts International, 47*(9-a), 3223.

Gould, R. (1965). Suicide problems in children and adolescents. *American Journal of Psychotherapy, 19,* 228–246.

Gould, R. (1972). *Child studies through fantasy.* New York: Quadrangle.

Greenfield, P. M., & Childs, C. P. (1977). Understanding sibling concepts: A developmental study of kin terms in Zinacantan. In P. Dasen (Ed.), *Cross-cultural Piagetian psychology.* New York: Gardner Press.

Greenspan, S. I. (1979). *Intelligence and adaptation: An integration of psychoanalytic and Piagetian developmental psychology.* New York: International Universities Press.

Gruber H. E., & Voneche J. J. (Eds.). (1977). *The Essential Piaget.* New York: Basic Books.

Grusec, J. E. (1973). Effects of co-observer evaluations on imitation: A developmental study. *Developmental Psychology, 8*(1), 141.

Hampshire, S., & Hart, H. L. A. (1958). Decision, intention, and certainty. *Mind, 67,* 1–12.

Harter, S. (1981). A model of intrinsic mastery motivation in children: Individual differences and developmental change. In W. A. Collins (Ed.), *Minnesota Symposium on Child Psychology (Vol. 14)*. Hillsdale, NJ: Lawrence Erlbaum.

Hartup, W. W. (1979). The social worlds of childhood. *American Psychologist, 34*(10), 944–950.

Hartup, W. W., & Coates, B. (1967). Imitation of a peer as a function of reinforcement from the peer group and rewardingness of the model. *Child Development, 38,* 1003–1016.

Hartup, W. W., Glazer, J., & Charlesworth, R. (1967). Peer reinforcement and sociometric status. *Child Development, 38,* 1017–1024.

Hegland, S. M., & Galejs, I. (1983). Developmental aspects of locus of control in preschool children. *Journal of Genetic Psychology, 143*(2), 229–239.

Hoffman, M. L. (1975). Developmental synthesis of affect and cognition and its implications for altruistic motivation. *Developmental Psychology, 11,* 607–622.

Hoffman, M. L. (1982). Development of prosocial motivation: Empathy and guilt. In N. Eisenberg (Ed.), *The development of presocial behavior* (pp. 281–313). New York: Academic Press.

Hulme, I. L., & Lunzer, K. A. (1966). Play, language and reasoning in subnormal children. *Journal of Child Psychology and Psychiatry, 7,* 107–123.

Husaini, B. A., & Neff, J. A. (1981). Social-class and depressive symptomatology—the role of life change events and locus of control. *Journal of Nervous and Mental Disease, 169*(10), 638–647.

Ianotti, R. J. (1978). Effect of role-taking experiences on role taking, empathy, altruism, and aggression. *Developmental Psychology 14*(2), 119–124.

Iwanaga, M. (1973). Development of interpersonal play structure in three, four, and five year-old children. *Journal of Research and Development in Education, 6,* 71–82.

Johnson, J. H., & Sarason, I. G. (1978). Life stress, depression and anxiety—internal-external-control as a moderator variable. *Journal of Psychosomatic Research, 22*(3), 205–208.

Jones, B. T. (1978). A longitudinal study of Piagetian conceptual development related to self concept and locus of control in elementary school children. *Dissertation Abstracts International; B: The Sciences and Engineering, 39*(8B), 4065.

Kagan, J. (1972). Do infants think? *Scientific American, 226,* 74–83.

Kalter, N., Alpern, D., Spence, R., & Plunkett, J. W. (1984). Locus of control in children of divorce. *Journal of Personality Assessment, 48*(4), 410–414.

Kane, B. (1979). Children's concepts of death. *The Journal of Genetic Psychology, 134,* 141–153.

Kant, I. (1781). Kritik der reinen Vernunft. In W. Kaufman (Ed.), *Philosophic classics. Bacon to Kant (Vol. 2)*. Englewood, NJ: Prentice-Hall, 1961.

Kashani, J. H., & Carlson, G. A. (1987). Seriously depressed preschoolers. *American Journal of Psychiatry, 144,* 348–350.

Kelley, R. V. (1973). Instructional objectives, learner personality and prediction of academic achievement. *Dissertation Abstracts International*, *34*(1-A), 186-187.

Klein, P. S., & Tzuriel, D. (1986). Preschoolers type of temperament as predictor of potential difficulties in cognitive functioning. *Israel Journal of Psychiatry and Related Sciences*, *23*(1), 49-61.

Kuhn, D. (1977). Conditional reasoning in children. *Developmental Psychology*, *13*(4), 342-353.

Kuhn, D., & Phelps, H. (1976). The development of children's comprehension of casual direction. *Child Development*, *47*(1), 248-251.

Kuhn, D., Nash, S. C., & Brucken, L. (1978). Sex role concepts of two- and three-year-olds. *Child Development*, *49*, 445-451.

Kun, A. (1977). Development of the magnitude-covariation and compensation schemata in ability and effort attributions of performance. *Child Development*, *48*, 862-873.

Kun, A. (1978). Evidence for preschoolers' understanding of causal direction in extended causal sequences. *Child Development*, *49*, 218-222.

Langer, E. J. (1975). The illusion of control. *Journal of Personality and Social Psychology*, *32*, 311-328.

Lawrence, E., & Winschel, J. (1975). Locus of control: Implications for special education. *Exceptional Children*, *41*, 483-490.

Lefcourt, H. M. (1976). Locus of control and response to aversive events. *Canadian Psychological Review-Psychologie Canadienne*, *17*(3), 202-209.

Lefcourt, H. M., Miller, H. M., Ware, E. E., & Sherk, D. (1981). Locus of control as a modifier of the relationship between stressors and moods. *Journal of Personality and Social Psychology*, *41*(2), 357-369.

Levin, H., & Turgeon, V. (1957). The influence of the mother's presence on children's doll-play aggression. *Journal of Abnormal Social Psychology*, *55*, 304-308.

Lewin, K. (1942). Time perspective and morale. In W. Goodwin (Ed.), *Civilian Morale* (pp. 48-70). Boston: Houghton Mifflin.

Licht, B. G., & Dweck, C. S. (1981). Determinants of academic achievement: The interaction of children's achievement orientations with skill area. Manuscript submitted for publication.

Lieberman, A. F. (1977). Preschooler's competence with a peer: relations with attachment and peer experience. *Child Development*, *48*, 1279-1287.

Linn, R. T., & Hodge, G. K. (1982). Locus of control in childhood hyperactivity. *Journal of Consulting & Clinical Psychology*, *50*(4), 592-593.

Maccoby, E. E., & Jacklin, C. N. (1974). *The psychology of sex differences*. Stanford, CA: Stanford University Press.

Maccoby, E. E., & Jacklin, C. N. (1980). Sex differences in aggression: A rejoinder and reprise. *Child Development*, *51*, 964-980.

Magnusson, D., Stattin, H., & Allen, V. L. (1985). Biological maturation and social development: A longitudinal study of some adjustment processes from mid-adolescence to adulthood. *Journal of Youth and Adolescence*, *14*, 267-283.

Mahler, M., Pine, F., & Bergman, A. (1975). *The psychological birth of the human infant*. New York: Basic Books.

Maier, S. F., Seligman, M. E. P., & Solomon, R. L. (1969). Pavlovian fear conditioning and learned helplessness. In B. A. Campbell & R. M. Church (Eds.), *Punishment*. New York: Appleton-Century-Crofts.

Main, M. (1973). Exploration, play, and cognitive functioning as related to child-mother attachment. *Unpublished doctoral dissertation*, John Hopkins University.

Main, M., & Cassidy, J. (1988). Categories of response to reunion with the parent at age 6: Predictable from infant attachment classifications and stable over a 1-month period. *Developmental Psychology, 24*(3), 415–426.

Main, M., Kaplan, N., & Cassidy, J. (1985). Security in infancy, childhood and adulthood: A move to the level of representation. *Monographs of the Society for Research in Child Development, 50*, 66–104.

Marshall, H. H., Weinstein, R. S., Middlestadt, S., & Brattesani, K. A. (1980). *"Everyone's smart in our class": Relationship between classroom characteristics and perceived differential teacher treatment*. Paper presented at the American Educators Research Association.

Mast, V. K., Fagen, J. W., Rovee-Collier, C. K., & Sullivan, M. W. (1980). Immediate and long-term memory for reinforcement context: The development of learned expectancies in early infancy. *Child Development, 51*(3), 700–707.

McCall, R. B., & McGhee, P. E. (1977). The discrepancy hypothesis of attention and affect in infants. In I. C. Uzgiris & F. Weizmann (Eds.), *The structuring of experience* (pp. 179–210). New York: Plenum.

McClelland, D. C., & McGown, D. R. (1953). The effect of variable food reinforcement on the strength of a secondary reward. *Journal of Comparative Physiology and Psychology, 46*, 80–86.

McClelland, D. C., Atkinson, J. W., Clark, R. A., & Lowell, E. L. (1953). *The achievement motive*. New York: Appleton-Century-Crofts.

McCord, W., McCord, J., & Howard, A. (1961). Familial correlates of aggression. *Journal of Abnormal and Social Psychology, 62*, 79–93.

McDevitt, J. B. (1985). The emergence of hostile aggression and its defensive and adaptive modifications during the separation-individuation process. In H. P. Blum (Ed.), *Defense and Resistance* (pp. 273–298). New York: International Universities Press.

McFall, R. M. (1982). A review and reformulation of the concept of social skills. *Behavioral Assessment, 4*, 1–35.

McIntire, M. S., Carol, C. R., & Strumpler, L. J. (1972). The concept of death in midwestern children and youth. *American Journal of Diseases of Children, 123*(6), 527–532.

Meacham, M. L., & Wiesen, A. E. (1969). *Changing classroom behavior.* Scranton, PA: International Textbook.

Melges, F. T., & Bowlby, J. (1969). Types of hopelessness in psychopathological process. *Archives of General Psychiatry, 20*, 690–699.

Melges, F. T., & Fougerousse, C. E. (1966). Time, sense, emotions, and acute mental illness. *Journal of Psychiatric Research, 4*, 127–140.

Miller, S. W. (1979). Controllability and human stress: Method, evidence, and theory. *Behaviour Research and Therapy, 17*, 287–304.

Minde, K. (1987). The relevance of infant psychiatry to the understanding of adult psychopathology. *Canadian Journal of Psychiatry, 32*, 513–517.

Mineka, S., & Hendersen, R. W. (1985). Controllability and predictability in acquired motivation. *Annual Review of Psychology, 36*, 495-529.

Mischel, W., Zeiss, R., & Zeiss, A. (1974). Internal-external control and persistence: Validation and implications of the Stanford Preschool Internal-External Scale. *Journal of Personality and Social Psychology, 29*, 265-278.

Morgan, G. A., & Ricciuti, H. N. (1967). Infant's responses to strangers during the first year. In B. M. Foss (Ed.), *Determinants of infant behavior. Vol. IV.* London: Methuen.

Murray, H. A. (1933). The effect of fear upon estimates of maliciousness of other personalities. *Journal of Social Psychology, 4*, 310-329.

Musatti, T. (1983). Peer interaction in pretend play. In M. Stamback, M. Barriere, L. Bonica, R. Maisonnet, T. Musatti, S. Rayna, & M. Verba (Eds.), *Among babies.* Paris: Presses Universitaires de France.

Nagy, M. (1948). The child's theories concerning death. *Journal of Genetic Psychology, 73*, 3-27.

Nekanda-Trepka, C. J. S., Bishop, S., & Blackburn, I. M. (1983). Hopelessness and depression. *British Journal of Clinical Psychology, 22*, 49-60.

Neubauer, P. B. (1987). The many meanings of play. *The Psychologic Study of the Child, 42*, 3-9.

Nicholls, J. G. (1978). The development of the concepts of effort and ability, perception of academic attainment, and the understanding that difficult tasks require more ability. *Child Development, 49*, 800-814.

Nicholls, J. G. (1979). Development of perception of own attainment and casual attributions for success and failure in reading. *Journal of Educational Psychology, 71*, 94-99. (a)

Nicholls, J. G. (1981). Striving to demonstrate amd develop ability: A theory of achievement motivation. Unpublished manuscript, Purdue University.

Nicholls, J. G., & Miller, A. T. (1985). Differentiation of the concepts of luck and skill. *Developmental Psychology, 21*, 76-82.

Norris, L. W. (1980). The development of locus of control in kindergarten children with the examination of race, sex, birth order, and child care: experiences in the preschool years. *DAI, 41*(12), 4679.

Ollendick, D. G. (1979). Locus of control and anxiety as mediating variables of locus of conflict in disadvantaged youth. *The Journal of Psychology, 101*, 23-25.

Olweus, D. (1979). Stability of aggressive reaction patterns in males: a review. *Psychological Bulletin, 86*(4), 852-875.

Olweus, D. (1980a). Familial and temperamental determinants of aggressive behavior in adolescent boys: A causal analysis. *Developmental Psychology, 16*, 644-660.

Olweus, D. (1980b). The consistency issue in personality psychology revisited – with special reference to aggression. *British Journal of Social and Clinical Psychology, 19*, 377-390.

Ornstein, A. (1981). Self-pathology in childhood: developmental and clinical considerations. *Psychiatric Clinics of North America, 4*(3), 435-453.

Overton, W. F., & Jackson, J. P. (1973). The representation of imagined objects in action sequences: A developmental study. *Child Development, 44*, 309-314.

Pagel, H. (1982). *The Cosmic Code*. New York: Simon & Schuster.

Paivio, A. (1970). On the functional significance of imagery. *Psychological Bulletin, 73*, 385–392.

Parens, H. (1979). *The development of aggression in early childhood*. New York: Aronson.

Parke, R. D. (1970). The role of punishment in the socialization process. In R. A. Hoppe, G. A. Milton, & E. C. Simmel (Eds.), *Early experiences and the processes of socialization*. New York: Academic Press.

Parke, R. D., & Deur, J. L. (1972). Schedule of punishment and inhibition. *Developmental Psychology, 7*, 266–269.

Parke, R. D., & Slaby, R. G. (1983). The development of aggression. In P. H. Mussen, J. H. Flavell, & E. M. Markman (Eds.), *Handbook of child psychology: Vol. 3. Cognitive development* (pp. 547–621). New York: Wiley.

Parkes, K. R. (1984). Locus of control, cognitive appraisal, and coping in stressful episodes. *Journal of Perspectives in Social Psychology, 46(3)*, 655–658.

Parsons, J. E., & Ruble, D. N. (1977). The development of achievement-related experiences. *Child Development, 48*, 1075–1079.

Parten, M. B. (1932). Social participation among pre-school children. *Journal of Abnormal and Social Psychology, 27*, 243–269.

Pastore, N. (1952). The role of arbitrariness in the frustration-aggression hypothesis. *Journal of Abnormal and Social Psychology, 47*, 728–731.

Patterson, B. R., McNeal, S., & Hawkins, N. (1967). Reprogramming the social environment. *Journal of Child Psychology and Psychiatry and Allied Disciplines, 8(3)*, 181–195.

Peller, L. (1954). Libidinal phases, ego development, and play. *Psychoanalytic Study of the Child, 9*, 178–198.

Perry, D. G., Perry, L. C., Bussey, K., English, D., & Arnold, G. (1980). Processes of attribution and children's self-punishment following misbehavior. *Child Development, 51*, 545–551.

Peterson, C., & Seligman, M. E. (1984). Casual explanations as a risk factor for depression: Theory and evidence. *Psychological Review, 91*, 347–374.

Peterson, L., & Hartmann, D. P. (1977). Developmental changes in effects of dependency and reciprocity cues on childrens' moral judgment and donation rates. *Child Development, 48(4)*, 1331–1339.

Phares, E. J. (1976). *Locus of control in personality*. NJ: General Learning Press.

Piaget, J. (1925). De quelques formes primitives de causalite chez l'enfant. *L'Annee Psychologie, 26*, 31–71.

Piaget, J. (1926). *The language and thought of the child*. New York: Harcourt, Brace.

Piaget, J. (1927). The child's conception of physical causality. In H. E. Gruber & J. J. Voneche (Eds.), *The essential Piaget*. New York: Basic Books.

Piaget, J. (1929). *The child's conception of physical causality*. London: Routledge & Kegan Paul.

Piaget, J. (1948). *The moral judgement of the child*. Glencoe, Ill.: Free Press.

Piaget, J. (1952). *The origins of intelligence in children*. New York: International Universities Press.

Piaget, J. (1954). *The origins of intelligence in children*. New York: Basic Books. (Original work published 1936).

Piaget, J. (1962). *Play, dreams, and imitation*. (C. Gattegno & F. N. Hodgson, Trans.). New York: Norton. (Original work published 1946).

Piaget, J., & Inhelder, B. (1975). *The origins of the idea of chance in children*. New York: Norton.

Plenk, A. M., & Hinchey, F. S. (1985). Clinical assessment of maladjusted preschool children. *Child Welfare, 64*(2), 127–134.

Plunkett, J. W., Klein, T., & Meisels, S. J. (1988). *Infant behavior and Development, 11,* 83–96.

Prawat, R. S., Grissom, S., & Parish, T. S. (1979). Affective development in children, grades 3 through 12. *Journal of Genetic Psychology, 135*(1), 37–49.

Radke-Yarrow, M., Cummings, E. M., Kuczynski, L., & Chapman, M. (1985). Patterns of attachment in two- and three-year-olds in normal families and families with paternal depression. *Child Development, 56,* 884–893.

Rholes, W. S., Blackwell, J., Jordan, C., & Walters, C. (1980). A developmental study of learned helplessness. *Developmental Psychology, 16*(6), 616–624.

Robins, L. N. (1978). Sturdy childhood predictors of adult antisocial behavior: Replications from longitudinal studies. *Psychological Medicine, 8,* 611–622.

Rogers, H., & Saklofske, D. H. (1985). Self-concepts, locus of control and performance expectations of learning disabled children. *Journal of Learning Disabilities, 18*(5), 273–278.

Rohwer, W. D., Jr. (1967). *Social class differences in the role of linguistic structures and paired associate learning: Elaboration and learning proficiency.* Final report, Bureau of Research, Office of Education, Berkeley, California: University of California.

Rosen, C. E. (1974). The effects of sociodramatic play on problem-solving behavior among culturally disadvantaged preschool children. *Child Development, 45,* 920–927.

Roth, S. (1975). Effects of noncontingent reinforcement on tasks of differing importance – facilitation and learned helplessness. *Journal of Personality and Social Psychology, 32*(4), 680–691.

Roth, S., & Kubal, L. (1975). Effects of noncontingent reinforcement on tasks of differing importance: facilitation and learned helplessness. *Journal of Personality and Social Psychology, 32,* 680–691.

Rothbart, M. K., & Derryberry, D. (1981). Development of individual differences in temperament. In M. E. Lamb & A. L. Brown (Eds.), *Advances in Developmental Psychology: Vol. 1* (pp. 39–101). Hillsdale, NJ: Lawrence Erlbaum.

Rothbart, M. K., & Derryberry, D. (1982). Theoretical issues in temperament. In M. Lewis & L. T. Taft (Eds.), *Developmental disabilities: Theory, assessment, and intervention* (pp. 383–400). New York: SP Medical and Scientific Books.

Rothbaum, F. (1980). Children's clinical syndromes and generalized expectations of control. *Advances in Child Development and Behavior, 15,* 207–246.

Rothbaum, F., Weisz, J. R., & Snyder, S. S. (1982). Changing the world and changing the self—a 2-process model of perceived control. *Journal of Personality and Social Psychology, 42*(1), 5–37.

Rothstein, A. (1981). Hallucinatory Phenomena in Childhood. *Journal of the Academy of Child Psychiatry, 20,* 623–635.

Rotter, J. B. (1966). Generalized expectancies for internal versus external control of reinforcement. *Psychological Monographs, 80*(1), 1–28.

Rubin, K., Fein, G. G., & Vandenberg, B. (1983). Play. In E. M. Hetherington (Ed.), P. H. Mussen (Series Ed.), *Handbook of child psychology: Socialization personality and social development (Vol. 4).* New York: Wiley.

Rubin, K. H., Maioni, T. L., & Hornung, M. (1976). Free play behavior in middle- and lower-class preschoolers: Partgen and Piaget revisited. *Child Development, 47,* 414–419.

Ruble, D. N., Parsons, J. E., & Ross, J. (1976). Self-evaluative responses of children in achievement settings. *Child Development, 47,* 990–997.

Rule, B. G., Nesdale, A. R., & McAra, M. J. (1974). Children's reactions to information about the intentions underlying an aggressive act. *Child Development, 45,* 794–798.

Rutter, M. (1987). The role of cognition in child development and disorder. *British Journal of Medical Psychology, 60,* 1–16.

Sackheim, H. A., & Wegner, A. Z. (1986). Attributional patterns in depression and euthymia. *Archives of General Psychiatry, 43*(1), 103–109.

Saltz, E., Dixon, D., & Johnson, J. (1977). Training disadvantaged preschoolers on various fantasy activities: Effects on cognitive functioning and impulse control. *Child Development, 48,* 367–380.

Sameroff, A. J., & Chandler, M. J. (1984). Reproductive risk and the continuum of caretaking casualty. In L. Grinspoon (Ed.), *Psychiatry Update (Vol. 3).* Washington, D.C.: American Psychiatric Press.

Schmidt, C., & Paris, S. F. (1978). Operativity and reversibility in children's understanding of pictorial sequences. *Child Development, 49*(1), 1219–1222.

Schneidman, E. S. (1966). Orientations toward death. In R. W. White (Ed.), *The study of lives* (pp. 201–227). New York: Atherton Press.

Schowalter, J. E. (1970). The child's reaction to his own terminal illness. In B. Schoenberg, A. C. Carr, D. Peretz, & A. H. Kutscher (Eds.), *Loss and grief: Psychological management in medical practice.* New York: Columbia University Press.

Schreier, H. A., & Libow, J. (1986). Acute phobic hallucinations in very young children. *Journal of the American Academy of Child Psychiatry, 25*(4), 574–578.

Schunk, D. H. (1983). Developing children's self-efficacy and skills: The roles of social comparative information and goal setting. *Contemporary Educational Psychology, 8*(1), 76–86.

Sears, R. R. (1961). Relation of early socialization. *Journal of Abnormal and Social Psychology, 63,* 466–492.

Seeman, M., & Evans, J. M. (1962). Alienation and learning in a hospital setting. *American Sociological Review, 27*(6), 772–782.

Seligman, M. E. P. (1975). *Helplessness: On depression, development and death.* San Francisco: Freeman.

Seligman, M. E. P., & Maier, S. F. (1967). Failure to escape traumatic shock. *Journal of Experimental Psychology, 74,* 1–9.

Seligman, M. E. P., & Peterson, C. (1986). A learned helplessness perspective on childhood depression: Theory and research. In M. Rutter, C. E. Izard, & P. B. Read (Eds.), *Depression in young people* (pp. 223–249). New York: Guilford.

Seligman, M. E. P., Kaslow, N. J., Alloy, L. B., Peterson, C., Tannenbaum, L., & Abramson, L. Y. (1984). Attributional style and depressive symptoms among children. *Journal of Abnormal Psychology, 93*(2), 235–238.

Shantz, D. W., & Voyandoff, D. A. (1973). Situational effects on retaliatory aggression at three age levels. *Child Development, 44,* 149–154.

Sheffield, F. D. (1961). Theoretical considerations in the learning of complex sequential tasks from demonstration and practice. In A. A. Lumsdaine (Ed.), *Student Response in Programmed Instruction* (pp. 13–32). Washington, D.C.: National Academy of Sciences – National Research Council.

Shultz, T. R. (1980). Development of the concept of intention. In W. A. Collins (Ed.), *Development of cognition, affect, and social relations. The Minnesota Symposia on Child Psychology (Vol. 13).* Hillsdale, NJ: Erlbaum.

Shultz, T. R. (1982a). Causal reasoning in the social and nonsocial realms. *Canadian Journal of Behavioral Science, 14*(4), 465–471.

Shultz, T. R. (1982b). Rules of Causal Attribution. *Monographs of the Society for Research in Child Development, 47*(1, Serial No. 194), 1–51.

Shultz, T. R., & Cloghesy, K. (1981). Development of recursive awareness of intention. *Developmental Psychology, 17*(4), 465–471.

Shultz, T. R., & Mendelson, R. (1975). The use of covariation as a principle of causal analysis. *Child Development, 46*(2), 394–399.

Shultz, T. R., & Shamash, F. (1981). The child's conception of intending act and consequence. *Canadian Journal of Behavioral Science, 13,* 368–372.

Shultz, T. R., Wells, D., & Sarda, M. (1980). Development of the ability to distinguish intended actions from mistakes, reflexes, and passive movements. *British Journal of Social and Clinical Psychology, 19,* 301–310.

Sigel, I. E., Saltz, E., & Roskind, W. (1967). Variables determing concept conversation in children. *Journal of Experimental Psychology, 74,* 471–475.

Singer, J. L. (1961). Imagination and waiting ability in young children. *Journal of Personality, 29,* 396–413.

Singer, J. L. (1973). *The Child's World of Make Believe.* New York: Academic Press.

Singer, J. L. (1977). Imagination and make-believe play in early childhood: Some educational implications. *Journal of Mental Imagery, 1,* 127–144.

Singer, J. L. (1979). Affect and imagination in play and fantasy. In C. Izard (Ed.), *Emotions in personality and psychopathology.* New York: Plenum.

Singer, J. L., & Singer, D. G. (1976). Imaginative play and pretending in early childhood. In A. Davids (Ed.), *Child personality and psychopathology.* New York: Wiley-Interscience.

Skinner, B. F. (1969). *Contingencies of reinforcement; a theoretical analysis.* New York: Appleton-Century-Croft.

Slade, B. B., Steward, M. S., Morrison, T. L., & Abramowitz, S. I. (1984). Locus of control, persistence, and use of contingency information in physically abused children. *Child Abuse & Neglect, 8,* 447–457.

Smilansky, S. (1968). *The effects of sociodramatic play on disadvantaged children: Preschool children.* New York: Wiley.

Smith, A. B., & Bain, H. (1978). Dependency in day-care and playcentre children. *New Zealand Journal of Educational Studies, 13*(2), 163–173.

Smith, P. K., & Green, M. (1975). Aggressive behavior in English nurseries and play groups: sex differences and response of adults. *Child Development, 46,* 211–214.

Smith, P. K., & Sydall, S. (1978). Play and non-play tutoring in preschool children: Is it play or tutoring which matters? *British Journal of Educational Psychology, 48,* 315–325.

Sommers, S. (1981). Emotionality reconsidered: the role of cognition in emotional responsiveness. *Journal of Personality and Social Psychology, 41,* 553–561.

Speece, M. W., & Brent, S. B. (1984). Children's understanding of death: A review of three components of a death concept. *Child Development, 55,* 1671–1686.

Spitz, R. A., & Wolf, K. M. (1946). Anaclitic depression. *Psychoanalytical Study of the Child, 2,* 313–342.

Sroufe, L. A., & Rutter, M. (1984). The domain of developmental psychology. *Child Development, 55,* 17–29.

Standahl, J. J. (1975). Verbal self-regulation of behavior by children with internal and external locus of control. *Dissertation Abstracts International; A: The Humanities and Social Sciences, 37,* 1296–1297.

Staub, E. (1971). The learning and unlearning of aggression. In M. Singer (Ed.) *The Control of Aggression and Violence* (pp. 93–124). New York: Academic Press.

Steinmetz, S. K. (1977). *The cycle of violence: Assertive, aggressive, and abusive family interaction.* New York: Praeger.

Stern, D. N., & Gibbon, J. (1978). Temporal expectancies of social behaviors in mother-infant play. In E. Thoman (Ed.), *Origins of the infant's social responsiveness* (pp. 409–429). New York: Erlbaum Press.

Stipek, D. (1981a). Children's perceptions of their own and their classmates' ability. *Journal of Educational Psychology, 3,* 404–410.

Stipek, D. (1981b). Social-motivational development in first-grade. *Contemporary Educational Psychology, 6,* 33–45.

Stipek, D. J., Roberts, T. A., & Sanborn, M. E. (1984). Preschool-age children's performance expectations for themselves and another child as a function of the incentive value of success and the salience of past performance. *Child Development, 55,* 1983–1989.

Strain, P. S., & Wiegernik, R. (1976). The effects of sociodramatic activities on social interaction among behaviorally disordered preschool children. *Journal of Special Education, 10,* 71–75.

Straus, M. (1980). Victims and aggressors in marital violence. *American Behavioral Scientist, 23*(5), 681–704.

Straus, M., & Hotaling, G. T. (Eds.) (1980). *The social causes of husband-wife violence.* Minneapolis: University of Minneapolis Press.

Strayer, J. (1980). A naturalistic study of empathic behaviors and their relation to affective states and perspective-taking skills in preschool children. *Child Development, 51,* 815–822.

Swanson, L. (1981). Locus of control and academic achievement in learning-disabled children. *The Journal of Social Psychology, 113,* 141–142.

Tennen, H., & Eller, S. J. (1977). Attributional components of learned helplessness and facilitation. *Journal of Personality and Social Psychology, 35*(4), 265–271.

Tesiny, E. P., Lefkowitz, M. M., & Gordon, N. H. (1980). Childhood depression, locus of control, and school achievement. *Journal of Educational Psychology, 72*(4), 506–510.

Thomas, A., & Chess, S. (1984). Genesis and evolution of behavior disorders: From infancy to early adult life. *American Journal of Psychiatry, 141,* 1–9.

Thomas, A., Chess, S., & Birch, H. G. (1968). *Temperament and behavior disorders in children.* New York: New York University Press.

Thomas, M. H., & Drabman, R. S. (1975). Toleration of real life aggression as a function of exposure to televised violence and age of subject. *Merrill-Palmer Quarterly, 21*(3), 227–232.

Thompson, R. A., & Lamb, M. E. (1982). Stranger sociability and its relationships to temperament and social experience during the second year. *Infant Behavior and Development, 5,* 277–287.

Tischler, C. L. (1980). Intentional self-destructive behavior in children under age ten. *Clinical Pediatrics, 19*(7), 451–453.

Tolor, A., Tolor, B., & Blumin, S. S. (1977). Self-concept and locus of control in primary-grade children identified as requiring special educational programing. *Psychological Reports, 40,* 43–49.

Topol, P., & Reznihoff, M. (1982). Perceived peer and family relationships, hopelessness and locus of control as factors in adolescent suicide attempts. *Suicide and Life-Threatening Behavior, 12*(3), 141–150.

Trad, P. (1986). *Infant depression: paradigms and paradoxes.* New York: Springer-Verlag.

Trad, P. (1987). *Infant and childhood depression: developmental factors.* New York: Wiley.

Trad, P. (1988). *Psychosocial scenarios for pediatrics.* New York: Springer-Verlag.

Trevarthen, C., & Hubley, P. (1978). Secondary intersubjectivity: Confidence, confiding and acts of meaning in the first year. In A. Lock (Ed.), *Action, gesture and symbol: The emergence of language* (pp. 183–229). London/New York: Academic.

Trivers, R. L. (1971). The evolution of reciprocal altruism. *Quarterly Review of Biology, 46,* 35–57.

Van Den Daele, L. (1970). Preschool intervention with social learning. *Journal of Negro Education, 39,* 296–304.

Van der Veen, F. (1965). The parent's concept of the family unit and child adjustment. *Journal of Counseling Psychology, 12*(2), 196–200.

Vandenburg, B. (1978). Play and development from an ethological perspective. *American Psychologist, 33,* 724–738.

Victor, J. B., Halverson, C. F., & Montague, R. B. (1985). Relations between reflection-impulsivity and behavioral impulsivity in preschool children. *Developmental Psychology, 21*(1), 141–148.

Vygotsky, L. (1967). Play and its role in the mental development of the child. *Soviet Psychology, 5,* 6–18.

Vygotsky, L. S. (1962). *Thought and Language.* Cambridge, MA: M.I.T. Press.

Waelder, R. (1933). The psychoanalytical theory of play. *Psychoanalytic Quarterly, 2,* 208–224.

Wallace, J. R., & Fonte, M. E. (1984). Piagetian and information processing approaches to concepts of chance and probability: relationships among methods, age, and locus of control. *The Journal of Genetic Psychology, 144,* 184–194.

Walters, R. H., & Parke, R. D. (1967). The influence of punishment and related disciplinary techniques on the social behavior of children: Theory and empirical findings. In B. A. Mahler (Ed.), *Progess in experimental personality research, Vol. 3.* New York: Academic Press.

Watson, J. S. (1966). The development of and generalization of "contingency awareness" in early infancy. *Merrill Palmer Quarterly, 17,* 123–125.

Watson, J. S., & Ramey, C. T. (1972). Reactions to response contingent stimulation in early infancy. *Merrill Palmer Quarterly, 18,* 219–227.

Watson, M. W. (1981). The development of social roles: A sequence of social-cognitive development. *New Directions for Child Development, 12,* 33–41.

Watson, M. W. (1986). The breadth of the appearance-reality distinction. In J. H. Flavell, F. L. Green, & E. R. Flavell (Eds.), Development of knowledge about appearance-reality distinction. *Monographs of the Society for Research in Child Development, 51*(1, Serial no. 212) 70–76.

Watson, M. W., & Fischer, K. W. (1980). Development of social roles in elicited and spontaneous behavior during the preschool years. *Developmental Psychology, 16,* 483–494.

Watson, M. W., & Fischer, K. W. (1977). A developmental sequence of agent use in late infancy. *Child Development, 48,* 828–836.

Weiner, B. (1979). A theory of motivation for some classroom experiences. *Journal of Educational Psychology, 71,* 3–25.

Weiner, B., Russell, D., & Lerman, D. The cognition-emotion process in achievement-related contexts. *Journal of Personality and Social Psychology, 37,* 1211–1220.

Weiner, I. B., & Ader, R. (1965). Direction of aggression and adaptation to free operant avoidance conditioning. *Journal of Personality and Social Psychology, 2,* 426–429.

Weisz, J. R. (1980). Autonomy, control, and other reasons why 'Mom is the greatest': a content analysis of children's Mother Day letters. *Child Development, 51,* 801–807.

Weisz, J. R. (1981). Illusory contingency in children at the state fair. *Developmental Psychology, 16,* 385–390.

Weisz, J. R., & Stipek, D. J. (1982). Competence, contingency, and the development of perceived control. *Human Development, 25,* 250–281.

Weisz, J. R., Yeates, K. O., & Robertson, D. (1981) Development of perceived contingency for skill and chance tasks (University of North Carolina at Chapel Hill, Chapel Hill, unpublished).

Werner, H., & Kaplan, B. (1963). *Symbol Formation.* New York: Wiley.

Weschler, D. (1955). *WAIS manual: Weschler Adult Intelligence Scale.* Psychological Corporation, New York.

White, E., Elsom, B., & Prawat, R. (1978). Children's conception of death. *Child Development, 49,* 307-310.

White, R. W. (1959). Motivation reconsidered: The concept of competence. *Psychological Review, 66,* 297-333.

White, S. H. (1965). Evidence for a hierarchical arrangement of learning processes. In L. P. Lipsitt & C. C. Cpiker (Eds.), *Advances in Child Development and Behavior (Vol. 2).* New York: Academic Press.

Wiehe, V. R. (1984). Self-esteem, attitude toward parents, and locus of control in children of divorced and non-divorced families. *Journal of Social Service Research, 8*(1), 17-28.

Wiehe, V. R. (1986). Loco parentis and locus of control. *Psychological Reports, 59*(1), 169-170.

Wine, J. D. (1982). Evaluation anxiety: A cognitive-attentional construct. *Series in clinical and community psychology: Achievement, Stress, and Anxiety,* 207-219.

Witelson, S. F. (1976). Sex and the single hemisphere: Specialization of the right hemisphere for spatial processing. *Science, 193,* 425-427.

Wolf, F. M., & Savickas, M. L. (1985). Time perspective and causal attributions for achievement. *Journal of Educational Psychology, 77*(4), 471-480.

Zahavi, S., & Asher, S. R. (1978). The effect of verbal instructions on preschool children's aggressive behavior. *Journal of School Psychology, 16*(2), 146-153.

Zahn-Waxler, C., & Radke-Yarrow, M. (1982). The development of altruism: Alternative research strategies. In N. Eisenberg-Berg (Ed.), *The development of prosocial behavior* (pp. 109-137). New York: Academic.

Zautra, A. J., Guenther, R. T., & Chartier, G. M. (1985). Attributions for real and hypothetical events: Their relation to self-esteem and depression. *Journal of Abnormal Psychology, 94*(4), 530-540.

NAME INDEX

SUBJECT INDEX